M000210062

Praise for *Dangerous Virtues*

We live in an upside-down world where good is rebranded as evil, and wrong is celebrated as right. John Koessler's bracing, relatable book is meant to reorient us to God's goodness so we can live with clarity, obedience, and true joy. *Dangerous Virtues* is a modern exploration of the seven deadly sins, calling readers to ask hard questions of the cultural norms that form our lives and churches while pointing us toward everyday moral choices that reflect the character of God.

MICHELLE VAN LOON
Author of *Becoming Sage: Cultivating Maturity, Purpose, and Spirituality at Midlife*

John Koessler, professor emeritus of pastoral studies at Moody Bible Institute, pens an honest, unsettling, and helpful book for all who have ears to hear. *Dangerous Virtues* shows its author to be experienced in the cure of souls. The good doctor makes a difficult but needed diagnosis of our culture: what we used to regard as vice is now virtue; "the seven deadly sins are now the seven dangerous virtues." Koessler's prescription is clear, attractive, and full of wisdom. Does he have a remedy for Christians? Christian virtue is choosing to live according to God's Word. But before we do this, we must embrace the gospel to learn who we are. Then, even though God in Christ has forgiven believers, sin is still very much with us. This medicine is not new, but it is biblical: we must put sin to death through the power of Jesus's death as we walk by faith relying on the Holy Spirit.

ROBERT A. PETERSON
Theologian and author of *The Assurance of Salvation: Biblical Hope for Our Struggles*

Everyone should read a book on the seven deadly sins, sins often sentimentalized, or, as John Koessler wisely notes, "rehabilitated." Our chronic hungers, encouraged by cultural erosion and technological obsession, must be recognized for what they are, then converted, retrained, and limited for the sake of Christian virtue. Gluttony, not just overeating, can also be overly careful eating; leisure used thoughtlessly easily becomes sloth, prosperity slips into greed, and a vision for social justice may fuel anger. As this colorfully written, biblically founded, well-researched book argues, sin, dressed respectably, infects everything. To be truly Christian, we need to know ourselves. This book is the opening to conviction.

ROSALIE DE ROSSET
Professor of Communications and Literature, Moody Bible Institute

DANGEROUS VIRTUES

How to
Follow
Jesus
When *Evil*
Masquerades
as Good

JOHN KOESSLER

MOODY PUBLISHERS

CHICAGO

© 2020 by
John Koessler

Published in association with Mark Sweeney & Associates

Edited by Kevin P. Emmert
Interior Design: Erik M. Peterson
Cover Design: Faceout Studio
Cover illustration of sheep copyright © 2019 by Nastasic / Getty Images (657039204). All rights reserved.
Cover illustration of wolf copyright © 2019 by nicoolay / Getty Images (184935577). All rights reserved.

All websites and phone numbers listed herein are accurate at the time of publication but may change in the future or cease to exist. The listing of website references and resources does not imply publisher endorsement of the site's entire contents. Groups and organizations are listed for informational purposes, and listing does not imply publisher endorsement of their activities.

Library of Congress Cataloging-in-Publication Data

Names: Koessler, John, 1953- author.
Title: Dangerous virtues : how to follow Jesus when evil masquerades as good / John Koessler.
Description: Chicago : Moody Publishers, 2020. | Includes bibliographical references. | Summary: "When sin is disguised as virtue, the path to cultivating righteousness becomes impossible. Dangerous Virtues examines how to recognize these seven deadly sins as they are subtly disguised in today's culture. Christians must develop a discerning eye in a world where good is called evil and evil called good"-- Provided by publisher.
Identifiers: LCCN 2020015689 (print) | LCCN 2020015690 (ebook) | ISBN 9780802419644 (paperback) | ISBN 9780802498564 (ebook)
Subjects: LCSH: Deadly sins. | Good and evil--Religious aspects--Christianity. | Virtues.
Classification: LCC BV4626 .K64 2020 (print) | LCC BV4626 (ebook) | DDC 241/.3--dc23
LC record available at https://lccn.loc.gov/2020015689
LC ebook record available at https://lccn.loc.gov/2020015690

Originally delivered by fleets of horse-drawn wagons, the affordable paperbacks from D. L. Moody's publishing house resourced the church and served everyday people. Now, after more than 125 years of publishing and ministry, Moody Publishers' mission remains the same— even if our delivery systems have changed a bit. For more information on other books (and resources) created from a biblical perspective, go to: www.moodypublishers.com or write to:

Moody Publishers
820 N. LaSalle Boulevard
Chicago, IL 60610

1 3 5 7 9 10 8 6 4 2

Printed in the United States of America

Contents

CHAPTER 1

Sin and the
Seven Dangerous Virtues

I n 1987, *Harper's Magazine* invited seven ad agencies to create a humorous campaign designed to rehabilitate the reputation of the seven deadly sins. The ad for lust pictured two silent film stars in a passionate embrace along with a headline that read, "Any sin that's enabled us to survive war, death, pestilence, and famine can't be called deadly." The ad's tagline read, "Lust, where would we be without it?" Another, for the Gluttony Society, showed a grossly obese man running in a race—or perhaps competing in the long jump—with the slogan, "Be all you can be." The ad for pride declared, "It's time to start feeling good about yourself—*really* good."

Although tongue in cheek, these ads accurately reflect the modern consensus when it comes to sin. We are sinners. We don't deny it. But most of the time, we don't think much about it. We don't seem to obsess about sin the way the ancients used to, at least not about our own sins. We don't punish ourselves or go to extreme measures to fight sin off. Most of the time, our sin feels more like a low-grade fever than it does a raging fire. Its presence is an ongoing irritation that may hinder us from being our best, but it doesn't keep us from functioning. Sin doesn't bother us that much, either. If anything, the fact that we are sinners serves as an escape clause when things go badly. "What did you think would happen?" we want to say. "We are imperfect people living in an imperfect world. Of course, we went off the rails." The fact that we are sinners is one of the few religious concepts upon which a majority of people agree. Most people identify with the label sinner.[1]

The ancients weren't as sanguine about the subject. The early Christian monastics went into the wilderness not only to pursue holiness but also to study their sinfulness. One monk, who probably lived in the fourth or fifth century, described the benefit of a life of solitude by pouring water into a cup and pointing out that its cloudy nature became clear after allowing it to stand for a time. "So it is with the man who lives among men. He does not see his own sins because of the turmoil," he said. "But when he is at rest, especially in the desert, then he sees his sins."[2]

Those early Christians analyzed sin and categorized the many ways it manifests itself. They were interested not only in identifying the specific acts that should be regarded as sinful but wanted to understand the internal dynamics that generated sinful behavior. The church's analysis and categorization of sin became so complex that the ordinary person who stumbles on its reflections may feel that such formulations read like tax documents produced by the IRS. But the fundamental questions that prompted theologians and philosophers to such deep and complicated reflection were often quite basic. They are the kinds of questions we all ask. What kind of behavior constitutes sin? How does sin arise within those who would rather not sin? Are some sins worse than others? And, of course, the most important question of all: what alternative is there to sin? At times, we all find ourselves, like the apostle Paul, puzzled by our behavior where sin is concerned (Rom. 7:15).

In the latter part of the fourth century, a monk named Evagrius of Pontus compiled a list of sins that people commonly commit. He didn't consider his list to be an exhaustive catalog of sinful behavior. The eight actions Evagrius singled out represented the main categories under which all other sins might fall. For this reason, they came to be known as "capital" sins. His list included gluttony, fornication, greed, sadness, anger, acedia (or sloth), vainglory, and pride. Later church leaders reduced the list to seven, reasoning that vainglory and pride were essentially the same.

No doubt, some of the items in the old monk's list seem odd to us. Hardly anyone today would call sadness a sin, let alone a capital sin. When someone's sadness is debilitating, we usually treat it as a disease. Likewise, gluttony seems to moderns to be a throwback to an age when food was scarce. We might think that it is unhealthy or perhaps rude, but we generally don't consider it to be a sin. Indeed, we usually don't think about it at all. I've heard only one sermon on gluttony in my life, and that was from a guest speaker during a chapel service while I was a student in seminary.

The athletically fit speaker told the audience that those of us who were overweight preached the gospel with our mouths but contradicted it with our lives (or more specifically, with our bodies). In the class that followed chapel that day, several of us were eager to know what our professor, a man of some girth, thought of the message. "Give me a moment," he said. "I am enjoying a Snickers bar." He chewed for a while and then in a wry tone declared: "All I have to say is that Proverbs 11:25 says, 'The liberal soul shall be made fat.'"

Acedia also seems out of place to most of us. After all, what's wrong with taking things a little easy? We don't even know what vainglory is, though we tend to recognize it in others. In those instances, we call it boasting. While we may be reluctant to categorize boasting as a sin, we do agree that it is bad form. Unless, of course, it appears on a resume. Fornication is still considered to be a sin by some. But hardly anybody fornicates anymore. Instead, people "make love." Love is widely regarded to be a good thing, and for many people making love is simply part of the dating ritual. Many today who stumble upon the Bible's denunciation of sexual sin wonder what all the fuss is about.

Contrary to the famous line uttered by Michael Douglas's character Gordon Gekko in the 1987 film *Wall Street*, most of us do not think that greed is good. But neither do we view it as a sin. At worst, I suppose, we consider it to be impolite, at least when it is displayed publicly. As long as greed is not put on display, people look at it as either thriftiness or success.

If you follow social media or drive the expressway, you already know that nobody believes that anger is a sin these days. We view it as an emotion. Actually, we now consider it to be a virtue, especially if it is exercised in the political sphere and is characterized as a "passion for justice." Indeed, most of the sins in this list have been turned upside down, so that what the ancients once regarded as sin modern people have relabeled to be less than sin. In an age that has learned to call evil good and good evil, the seven deadly sins are now the seven dangerous virtues.

—

Why do we think so differently from previous generations about sin? One reason is that we have radically different notions about virtue in our day. Moderns think as little about virtue as they do about sin in the traditional sense. The word seems outdated. Virtue sounds more like something that would have concerned our Victorian great-grandparents. So before we go any further, we should unpack the idea.

The notion of virtue is indeed an ancient one. In his *Nichomachean Ethics*, the Greek philosopher Aristotle saw virtue as the pattern of right behavior that characterizes a person. Virtue is a habit of life that moves one in the right direction. Vice is the same, only moving one in the opposite direction. Although the *term* may seem archaic, the *idea* of virtue is not, if we understand it as a preferred pattern of life. We may have dropped the philosophical language as a culture, but we still have strong feelings about the way people should live. If you doubt this, spend a few hours reading through the opinions expressed on your favorite social media feed. We do not all agree on the standard of what is considered good, but enough of us have strong opinions about what goodness looks like that we regularly criticize those who don't measure up to our standard. However, contemporary interest in virtue seems to be primarily negative. Our ideas about what is good do not necessarily serve as a basis for self-examination and personal improvement. Often, they merely provide the grounds for carping against others who fall short of our standard.

The ancient idea of virtue grew from a desire to overcome the human disposition that the Bible labels sin. This classical understanding of virtue assumed the need for improvement. Consequently, the quest for virtue required not only an understanding of its opposite but a sense of personal accountability. Not only has our downgraded sense of sin snuffed out interest in this ancient idea of virtue, but it has also seriously degraded contemporary notions of what it means to be human. "No modern formulation of humanness comes close to the virtue-and-vice tradition in capturing both the grandeur and the fatally flawed nature of human existence," Os Guinness has observed. "Modern views, instead, tend to be flippant about vice and reduce its seriousness to a yawn or a snicker."[3]

For Christians, God is the key component in any notion of virtue. He is also the key component in any notion of sin. Virtue doesn't just involve the measure of what *we* think is good as individuals. It is more than the community standard. In the Christian view, God is both the measure and the measurer of what constitutes genuine virtue. That same measure provides the dividing line that separates sin from virtue. It is popular to treat sin and virtue as if they were merely matters of subjective judgment. This view regards sin as a violation of one's individual standard or that of the community. The popular measure used to determine what constitutes sin is a movable scale and one that assumes the more lenient the measure, the more enlightened the standard. Such a view reduces many of the things that used to be called sins to exercises in bad taste, or at worst, judges them to be little more than a matter of gross insensitivity. In some cases, it removes many of the thoughts and practices that were once called sins from the category of sin altogether. They are choices, alternative lifestyles, or if they are negative, simply mistakes. The fatal flaw in this perspective is its exclusion of God. It is the same flaw that has corrupted our notion of virtue. Where there is no God, there is no sin. Where there is no God, there is no virtue, either. There are only privately or commonly held standards. What renders an action a sin is that it is ultimately committed against God.

David understood this. In Psalm 51:4, he declared, "Against you, you only, have I sinned and done what is evil in your sight; so you are right in your verdict and justified when you judge." This is an astonishing statement, given the events that prompted it. David committed adultery with Bathsheba. He arranged the murder of Bathsheba's husband, Uriah, after he learned that she had become pregnant. Theologian Cornelius Plantinga Jr. explains, "All sin has first and finally a Godward force."[4]

Virtue or goodness also has God as its primary reference point. Theologian John Murray observed that the essence of human virtue is "to be like God in the sense of reflecting his image in knowledge, righteousness, and holiness."[5] Or as Jesus puts it, no one is good but God. Virtue is what we were made for. It is a life that reflects our design as creatures made in the image of the God who is Himself good and the source of all that can be rightly called good. But as Jesus' response to the man who called Him a "good" teacher implies, we can't think about personal goodness or virtue without also taking our own sin into account. Any possibility of true goodness depends ultimately upon God. We must receive goodness as a gift before we adopt it as a practice.

—

Perhaps all of this sounds too abstract and detached for ordinary people like us. It's one thing for theologians and philosophers to debate about sin and virtue. Why should we concern ourselves with such matters? We have jobs to go to and bills to pay. We mow the lawn and drive the kids to school. What does any of this have to do with the real world in which we live? The answer is that sin and virtue lie at the heart of everything we do. Our ideas of sin and virtue shape the way we work at our job, live in our neighborhood, and treat the members of our family.

What is more, these matters are a deep concern for us. Sin and virtue drive the storylines behind the television programs and movies we watch. Our law courts are backlogged with cases in which the parties involved dispute with one another over these same concerns. We may use different language when we talk about sin and virtue. We may speak of "doing the right thing" or talk about what people "ought" to do. But philosopher Charles Taylor captures the importance these ideas hold for us when he describes our assumptions about these issues as "moral and spiritual intuitions" that express "strong evaluations" about the things "that make life worth living."[6]

We also seem to know intuitively when others have crossed a line. We may not agree about what is right, but nearly every one of us has a kind of moral radar that is hypersensitive to those who do something we consider wrong. C. S. Lewis called this intuition the "law of human nature," or the "rule of fair play," and characterizes it as an almost instinctive appeal to an unspoken common standard that we expect others to know and observe.[7] According to Lewis, this way of thinking is most evident when people quarrel with one another. It is a way of thinking that is as common among children as it is with adults. The rule of fair play is that inner sense that the person who transgresses against us should have known better. Suppose you are at the theater and leave your seat to buy popcorn. The line is long, and you are beginning to worry that the film is about to start. You would feel irritated if someone jumped the line and cut in front of you just as you came to the counter. You would feel an even greater instant sense of outrage upon returning to your seat to find that someone else was sitting in it. In such cases, we instinctively measure the behavior of others by the golden rule (Matt. 7:12). We say, "How would you like it if I treated you that way?"

Lewis goes on to point out that most of the time when we take someone to task for such offenses, they rarely reject the standard. "Nearly always he tries to make out that what he has been doing does not really go against the standard, or that if it does there is some special excuse," Lewis explains. "He pretends there is some special reason in this particular case why the person who took the seat first should not keep it, or that things were quite different when he was given a bit of orange, or that something turned up which lets him off keeping his promise."[8]

However, our moral radar seems to operate on only one band. We are hypersensitive to the transgressions of others but find it difficult to see our own. Not only do we disagree with the ancient consensus of the church about the gravity of our sins, but we are also strangely comforted by its universal presence. For some of us, the comfort we take in knowing we are sinners is the kind that a poor student might take who places their trust in the grading curve. We reason that if sin is normal, then we are normal. Even if there is something wrong with us, we can at least say that it is only your average, garden variety of wrong. Everybody suffers from it. Surely God won't penalize *everybody*.

Others treat sin the same way they do high cholesterol. They know that if they ignore it, things will go badly. But they hope that if they take certain basic measures, it can be kept under control. This approach to sin takes two primary forms: one is medical, and the other is athletic. The medical model sees sin as a kind of disease. The athletic model approaches sin like a weakness that can be remedied through discipline. Either view makes sin seem manageable. If sin is a sickness, it can be cured through treatment. If it is a weakness, that weakness can be eliminated with training.

One of the appeals of the medical model of sin is that it alleviates the moral pressure that comes with an awareness of sin. So far, I have had two major illnesses in my life. When I was a child, I contracted polio. As an adult, I was diagnosed with a form of cancer. I felt bad on both occasions, but I did not feel responsible.

I knew that something was wrong with me, but I did not think that I was at fault. Jesus Himself seemed to give credence to the medical model when, after being criticized for eating with tax collectors and sinners, He observed, "It is not the healthy who need a doctor, but the sick" (Matt. 9:12).

Many problems like addiction that we used to consider to have a moral component are treated as if they were only diseases. Others, like homosexuality, which used to be considered a moral problem or a social disorder, have been normalized. The medical model of sin is appealing because it seems to mitigate human responsibility and provides a familiar frame of reference for understanding how sin works. What is more, although sin is a spiritual condition, it does have qualities that seem organic. Like certain medical conditions or genetic defects, sin is passed on from one generation to another (Ps. 51:5). The Bible speaks of sin as something that is "alive" (Rom. 7:9). In Romans 7:18, the apostle Paul characterizes sin as something that is "in" him. More specifically, according to this verse, it is the "not good" that is in him.

The appeal of the athletic model of sin is its promise of improvement. The athletic approach to sin seems to imply that we can replace sin with virtue merely by applying the right combination of willpower and methodology. The apostle Paul seems to endorse it when he employs athletic imagery to describe the Christian life. He says that the Christian life is a race and that those who run it must go into "strict training" (1 Cor. 9:25).

According to Paul, discipline and effort are not the only elements needed to deal with the problem of sin. Sin is more than the absence of positive qualities, and virtue is more than muscle memory. Sin is a living force that resides within us (Rom. 7:17). The apostle even gives sin's location. It dwells "in my sinful nature" (v. 18). Flesh, in this case, is not a physiological term. It does not mean the skin that covers our bones. It is not organic in that sense. Rather, it is organic in an altogether different way. Sin is a force that is integrated into our nature. As New Testament scholar Handley Moule so vividly puts it, "The intruder has occupied the whole dwelling, and every part of it is infected."[9]

When Paul employs the term "flesh" in this way, it serves as a synonym for sin itself. Flesh, in this sense, is the sin that dwells in me. This biblical language hints at sin's point of origin. In one sense, sin is an intruder into God's creation. All that God created was "good" (Gen. 1:4, 10, 12, 18, 21, 25, 31). This "good" creation included humanity. Sin did not originate with God. As theologian Herman Ridderbos explains, "It is unmistakable that sin is not a cosmic but an ethical quantity, i.e., that it is not an original principle standing independently against God to which the world and man have fallen prey apart from their own will, but that it has entered into the world through man."[10] As the cartoon strip character Pogo observed, "We have met the enemy, and he is us."

Sin has another organic quality. It has physical consequences. These consequences extend beyond human beings to creation itself. As Paul puts it in Romans 8:20, creation has been "subjected to frustration" as a result of Adam's sin. This euphemistic language is a nod to the judgment pronounced by God in Genesis 3:17–18: "Cursed is the ground because of you; through painful toil you will eat food from it all the days of your life. It will produce thorns and thistles for you, and you will eat the plants of the field." It is not only ourselves but the world in which we live that has been affected by Adam's sin. To use the stark language of Genesis, creation is under a curse. Everything in it is subject to change and decay. Even the rocks and hills, which seem so firm and immovable to us, wear away in time.

Sin's universal consequence is death. Cornelius Plantinga Jr. notes, "The association of sin with physical and spiritual death runs like a spine through Scripture and Christian tradition."[11] When Adam was commanded not to eat of the forbidden tree, the Lord warned, "You are free to eat from any tree in the garden; but you must not eat from the tree of the knowledge of good and evil, for when you eat from it you will certainly die" (Gen. 2:16–17). Physical death offers universal proof of human sinfulness. Death is the objective evidence that we are "in Adam" and subject to the penalty for refusing to heed God's warning (1 Cor. 15:22). Through Adam, "death came to all people" (Rom. 5:12).

In Scripture, death is more than a physical condition. Death is also a pattern of living. The second-century handbook of the Christian life known as the *Didache* begins, "There are two ways, one of life and one of death, and there is a great difference between these two ways."[12] As might be expected, the way of death described in this work includes sinful deeds. Among them are murder, adultery, magic arts, sorcery, robbery, lying, hypocrisy, duplicity, deceitfulness, pride, malice, stubbornness, greed, abusive language, jealousy, arrogance, pride, and boastfulness. We would probably agree that most of the items in this list are unbecoming for someone who claims to follow Christ. We could also see how living such a life would lead to spiritual problems, although death might seem like an extreme penalty to some of us for attitudes that we normally regard as rude behavior or personality flaws. But there is more to the way of death than behaviors that warrant the penalty of death. The items mentioned in the *Didache* are drawn from the New Testament vice lists that describe the acts of the flesh (Gal. 5:19–21; Eph. 5:3–5; 1 Cor. 6:9–11). More than a Christian "don't" list, these New Testament passages provided Christians with a kind of mirror that showed how the spiritually dead live. They would have recognized what they saw because the attitudes and actions included in these lists were prominent features of their old way of life (Eph. 4:22). In other words, the "way of death" might more accurately be called the "way of the dead." It is a mode of existence.

More than this, these vice lists, when contrasted with the catalog of Christian virtues that often accompany them, make a powerful statement about the nature of Christ's life (Gal. 5:22–25; Eph. 4:32–5:2). Like all of creation, we are leaning into redemption. This is the essential point of the virtue lists in the New Testament. They are not meant to serve as a grocery list of good behaviors. The standard of behavior described in these passages is a mirror as much as it is a measure. They remind us of who we are and of what is possible for those who are alive in Christ. In other words, they describe the way of the living. Good is something we do, but thanks to Jesus Christ, it is also what we are. As far as our sinful nature goes, the part of us that is inclined to shake its fist at God and that the apostle calls the flesh, there is no good in us (Rom. 7:18). But believers have another force that determines the contour of their lives. This is the transforming work of Christ, which enables us "to become the righteousness of God" (2 Cor. 5:21). Theologians use the word *sanctification* to describe this work. It is progressive, cooperative, and imparted to us by the Holy Spirit. Sanctification is progressive. It does not happen at once. We grow in grace and add to our virtues. It is cooperative in the sense that we have a role to play in this transformation process through our obedience and practice. But sanctification depends upon the finished work of Jesus Christ and the empowerment of His indwelling Spirit. We are not earning our righteousness through these efforts. We are bringing into personal experience the righteousness that has been given to us as a gift by God's grace.

Even though we may sometimes slip into old patterns of thinking and acting, we are fundamentally different from the people we once were. Indeed, according to Romans 6:11, all those who are in Christ are not dead at all but "alive to God." When this verse tells us to "reckon" ourselves dead to sin, it is not urging us to think positively about ourselves. In the apostle's day, this was banker's language. What Paul calls believers to do is to make "a deliberate and sober judgment on the basis of the gospel."[13] We are urged to bank on the fact that our relationship both to sin and to God have fundamentally changed.

This means that virtue is more than a matter of what we do. Ultimately, it is a function of who we are. In the Christian life, *being* always precedes *doing*. To make such a distinction does not eliminate the necessity of choice or action. Virtue is not automatic. If it were, we would not need to be told to "add" virtue to our faith (2 Peter 1:5). But neither is virtue natural, at least as far as the flesh is concerned. Virtue is the disposition of our new nature in Christ. We might describe it as the power of God, which tends toward life. Virtue is that power that comes from God and that provides "everything we need for a godly life through our knowledge of him who called us by his own glory and goodness" (2 Peter 1:3). In his commentary on 2 Peter 1:3, John Calvin described it as something "over and above the common natural order."[14] We access this power through faith because the knowledge of it can be found only in those "very great and precious promises" recorded in Scripture.

In other words, virtue is a matter of acting in accordance with our God-given new nature. But before we can act upon these promises, we must first hear and believe them. Or to put it another way, virtue in the Christian realm is a matter of choosing to live in a way that is consistent with who we are in Christ by God's power. Before we can live this way, we must first be told who we are. This is the function of the gospel and God's Word in general.

—

Understanding the nature of virtue also enables us to truly understand sin. Sin is what virtue looks like after it has been twisted. Satan's false narrative in the garden of Eden implied that ignoring God's prohibition about eating from the forbidden tree could be a path to virtue. "You will not certainly die," the serpent assured the woman. "For God knows that when you eat from it your eyes will be opened, and you will be like God, knowing good and evil" (Gen. 3:4–5).

This explains the nature of sin's appeal, at least in part. Sin is a distortion of goodness. When we sin, we are often attempting to achieve a legitimate goal by illegitimate means. Sometimes the means that is presented to us seems to offer a shortcut. We think that if we throw off the restraints that God has placed upon us, we will obtain our ultimate desire more quickly. At other times, as in Eve's case, it is a matter of bait and switch. What Satan promised Eve was good—the possibility of being like God—but what he actually offered her was the opposite. His promise was a lie, and Eve was deceived by it (Gen. 3:13; 1 Tim. 2:14).

We might conclude from this that sin is merely a misguided attempt to get what God has promised us and that those who succumb to it are only spiritual victims of a cosmic trickster. But God's evaluation sends a different message. Satan is indeed a deceiver, but sin is also an act of rebellion. Paul's clarification in 1 Timothy 2:14 that Adam "was not the one deceived" places human sin squarely within the framework of conscious rebellion against God. Whatever Adam's motive may have been for ignoring what he knew to be true when he partook of the forbidden fruit, he knew what he was doing. Adam's action was not an error; it was a sin. However, Paul makes it just as clear that Eve's deception did not mitigate her guilt. Even though Eve was genuinely deceived by Satan, she "became a sinner" when she acted in error.

In general, our thinking about both sin and virtue is backward. We think more of individual sins than we do of sin. We treat virtue the same way. We tend to see virtue as a collection of righteous actions. Our concern when it comes to sin is that it will grow. Small infractions will become larger. Anger will accelerate until it becomes murder. Lust will take control and lead to adultery. According to Jesus' teaching in the Sermon on the Mount, sin moves in the opposite direction. It does not start small and increase. Those sins that we usually treat as minor infractions bloom from the same root as those we think of as large. Sinful anger springs from a murderous heart, not the other way around (Matt. 5:22). A lustful gaze is the offspring of an adulterous desire (Matt. 5:27–28). This does not mean that there is no difference between thought and action, or even that every sin is the same. Angry words are not the same as a shotgun blast to the head, though some might argue that both can be equally destructive in their own way. They might even say that between the two, the effects of someone's cruel words might last longer.

If the punishments described in the Law of Moses tells us anything about this matter, they reveal that God does not treat every sin the same. As far as individual actions go, there are greater sins and lesser ones. Even Jesus used the language of comparison when talking about sin (John 19:11). Theologian G. C. Berkouwer observes, "It is simply an undeniable fact that Scripture makes various distinctions and speaks of several 'degrees' of sin."[15] Those who want to place every act of disobedience on par with every other act of disobedience do so in the hope that it will heighten awareness of sin by magnifying the sinful character of the smaller act. Ironically, this way of thinking about sin often has the opposite effect. Moral egalitarianism tends to desensitize us to the gravity of sin. Actions that we used to consider grave sins are now simply "struggles" and in some cases, even acceptable behavior. We fear that condemning the greater sin when we are guilty of so-called lesser sins is hypocritical.

Sin is impartial. We are all equally guilty of sinning. But this does not mean that we are equal in our practice of it. A child is a sinner as much as an adult but is not as accomplished. Sin, like virtue, has an expandable quality.

But it is not enough to merely catalog our actions. Too often, when we categorize sin, we are looking for loopholes that will excuse us. Our tendency to sort sinful actions into those that are greater and lesser does not always spring from a desire to understand the depth of our failure. It often springs from a desire to rationalize away what we have done. We are like Lot when he begged for permission to ignore God's command to flee to the mountains: "Look, here is a town near enough to run to, and it is small. Let me flee to it—it is very small, isn't it? Then my life will be spared" (Gen. 19:20). When we take refuge in the smallness of what we have done, we fail to see that the difference in size means only that what we have done is a sprout from the same root as its larger kin. The problem of sin is deeper than the individual act. Even when we manage to avoid a specific sinful act, it does not mean we have evaded the sin that prompts it.

We treat virtue the same way that we do sin, looking at it through an accountant's eyes as an accumulation of good individual actions. Many people treat goodness the way they do their IRA, hoping to store up enough to counterbalance the bad they have done. Christians can also fall into this error by assuming that their relationship with God is only as secure as their daily track record of performance. If it's been a good day, they feel that they can approach Him with confidence. If not, they may try to balance things about by performing a few righteous acts so they can approach God with something in hand.

Righteousness or virtue has the same expansive quality that sin does. When Jesus describes the true nature of sin in the Sermon on the Mount, He also exposes the true nature of righteousness. Righteousness is not an accumulation of actions that can be classified as good but the other way around. What Jesus says is true of our speech also applies to our actions: "A good man brings good things out of the good stored up in him, and an evil man brings evil things out of the evil stored up in him" (Matt. 12:35). Righteousness in the Christian life is not a collection of good acts that balances out our bad deeds. Righteous actions spring from righteousness. Individual acts reflect the nature of those who do them. We have been made righteous to be righteous. Those who come to Jesus Christ in faith do not lose their capacity to sin. They gain the capacity to obey. This new ability springs from a changed nature, which is a reflection of their new standing before God. The Christian can do good because he or she has been made good through the blood of Jesus Christ.

This is a book about sin. In particular, it is a book about those sins that the church has traditionally labeled the seven deadly sins. What I will be talking about in the following pages is much more than a list. It is a kind of Rosetta Stone. We are living in an age when the seven deadly sins have become the seven deadly virtues. By focusing on these sins, we can see how our culture's ideas about what is right have gone dangerously wrong. But more importantly, we will also discover something about ourselves. Like those ancient monks did, we are about to embark on a journey of self-discovery that will take us to the trailhead where the sin in our lives begins. It is a difficult journey, fraught with perils. But sin is not our ultimate destination. This is a book about virtue or goodness as much as it is a book about sin. By considering the alternative to these deadly sins, we will discover much more than a way of life. If we look at them through the lens of Christ and His saving work, we will see the way of the living.

QUESTIONS FOR DISCUSSION:

1. How would you define virtue?

2. In what ways have you seen our culture's ideas about what is good change during your lifetime?

3. What is a biblical definition of virtue?

CHAPTER 2

Love:
The Seduction of Desire

I first learned about sex from my father. The lesson came in the form of a brief hallway conversation as he was in transit from his bedroom to the bathroom. I don't think my age was even in double digits at the time. I don't recall who initiated the conversation, though I suspect it was in response to a question I had asked. My father compared sex to a loaded gun and emphasized the need to be careful. "It's like a pistol," he said. "When it goes off, you can't stop it." I didn't understand much of what he said. The whole thing sounded pretty unappealing to me at the time. I was sure I would never want to have sex with anyone. I was wrong, of course. I didn't know it then, but the sexual revolution was just getting started. I turned sixteen in 1969, the summer that Woodstock happened. At the time, I was just a kid growing up in the rust belt of the Midwest, too young and too far away to attend the event whose posters promised "three days of peace and music." It turned out to be three days of sex, drugs, and rock and roll. Woodstock was the watershed event that showed how far the counterculture of the '60s had edged its way into the mainstream of popular consciousness. Staid newscasters in white shirts and ties covered it on the national news and pondered its cultural significance. Singer Joni Mitchell, who had been unable to attend because of a scheduled appearance on the *Dick Cavett Show*, wrote a hymn of praise that compared the music festival to Eden. More than a concert, Woodstock turned out to be the iconic moment of my generation. Boomers have been talking about it ever since.

Woodstock was the capstone of the movement that began two years earlier on the opposite coast when thousands of young people moved to San Francisco during the "summer of love." Forty-five years later, Country Joe McDonald would characterize the values of the era with these words: "They all want sex. They all want to have fun. Everyone wants hope. We opened the door, and everybody went through it, and everything changed after that."[1] During the summer of love, sex and love were synonymous. The sexual revolution changed not only the shape of sexual morals for a large part of the culture, but also our view of the place of sexual desire in human experience. Dale Kuehne, professor of ethics, economics, and the common good at Saint Anselm College observes, "There was no assumption until the 20th century that in order to lead the best, deepest, most fulfilling relational life, you needed to be in a sexual relationship."[2] Kuehne notes that this false assumption has caused some Christians today to question whether the Bible's teaching about sexuality and sexual practice is "good news."

But the sexual revolution, which was such a feature of the summer of love, did not usher in an age of fun and hope. Twenty-seven years after Woodstock, Joni Mitchell's song "Sex Kills" lamented injustice, greed, and the spread of the AIDS epidemic. Those who participated in the sexual revolution went looking for love and found death instead.

In Mitchell's song, sex is not the problem; it is a victim. She portrays sex as a tool that marketers use to exploit others. She is right when she says that sex sells. We are surrounded by sexual images that are used to sell everything from soap to shoes. What is more, the intended audience for these sexualized images has gotten younger with each passing decade. Author and activist Jean Kilbourne notes that images that would have once been considered pornographic are now commonly found in family magazines, on television, on billboards, and on non-pornographic internet sites. "Today's children are bombarded with graphic sexual content that they cannot fully process or understand and that can even frighten them."[3] The aim of these ads is to arouse a different kind of lust in children. "These sexual images aren't intended to sell our children on sex—they are intended to sell them on shopping," Kilbourne explains. "This is the intent of the marketers—but an unintended consequence is the effect these images have on real sexual desire and real lives."[4]

Joni Mitchell was right in another respect. Sex isn't the problem. The problem is desire and the unrealistic expectations that are born of our desire. The biblical word for this is *lust*. Sin entered human experience through common desire. Genesis 3:6 says, "When the woman saw that the fruit of the tree was good for food and pleasing to the eye, and also desirable for gaining wisdom, she took some and ate it. She also gave some to her husband, who was with her, and he ate it." The appetites mentioned in this verse are commonplace. The forbidden fruit was "good for food." In other words, the tree was edible. The tree was also appealing to the eye. The tree appeared to be "desirable for gaining wisdom." Like the original temptation, sexual lust is rooted in legitimate desire. Sexual desire is not wrong in itself. It is part of our biological and psychological design. But like all other appetites, this hunger can and must be controlled. Appetites can be misdirected or abused. We can be selfish and even perverse in our attempts to gratify them.

Desire can be dangerous, and few desires are more dangerous than this one. Sexual lust is quickly ignited, and once inflamed is not easily extinguished. The fact that sexual desire is ordinary does not mean that it is safe. My father's inept explanation of how sex works might not have been age-appropriate, but he was right to sound a note of warning. When we treat sex frivolously, it can be destructive to both body and soul (1 Cor. 6:18–20). Perhaps the most damaging effect of the sexual revolution was the way it trivialized sexual desire, removing sexual intercourse from the realm of the sacred and treating it as little more than a pleasurable bodily function. Sex is pleasurable, and it does involve the body. But sex is also more than this. Indeed, it is the fact that sex involves the body that makes it sacred because it means that sex involves the whole person. When we engage in sexual intercourse, we not only join our body with another, we join our whole self with another whole self. We unite with another person in such a way that the two become one. Paul explains in 1 Corinthians 6:15–16, "Do you not know that your bodies are members of Christ himself? Shall I then take the members of Christ and unite them with a prostitute? Never! Do you not know that he who unites himself with a prostitute is one with her in body? For it is said, 'The two will become one flesh.'" The language the apostle uses when speaking of fornication in these verses implies a spiritual as well as a physical reality.

Pornography objectifies the person whose image incites our lust. Similarly, when we yield to sexual lust, we objectify ourselves. When we indulge in sexual lust in its various forms, we relate to ourselves as if we were only a body and nothing more. Sexual desire is normal and holy. Sexual lust happens when normal sexual desire moves in a selfish and self-destructive direction.

According to theologian Helmut Thielicke, before the Renaissance, the boundaries that defined both sex and marriage were public rather than private. As he puts it, "they were a matter for the family and clan."[5] Individual love was a factor, but Thielicke observes that love was treated more as a consequence than a presupposition. The modern era flipped this. Instead of expecting love to develop within the confines of marriage, people married based on an attraction they already experienced. This does not mean that attraction was not a factor before the sexual revolution. The dramatic tension in the Old Testament love story between Jacob and Rachel revolves around the fact that Jacob loved Rachel and not her sister Leah. The Scriptures make it clear that this love story began with a powerful physical attraction (Gen. 29:17). The difference in the perspective of the ancients is seen in Jacob's reaction after he discovers that he has been tricked into marrying Leah instead of Rachel. He does not demand a divorce, nor does he fail to regard Leah as his wife.

The point here is not that attraction is irrelevant in marriage but that there is more to marriage than sexual attraction. "It would be stupid to think that Christian ethics wants selfless, ministering love of neighbor to replace eros," Thielicke rightly observes. "The one who marries with no erotic feeling but simply out of neighborly love and because of the other's need will bring unhappiness to them both, as we have noted in another context."[6]

The seduction of human love by the ethos of lust has only intensified since Thielicke made his observation in the mid-1970s. But the sensualism of the sexual revolution, epitomized by the popular slogan "if it feels good, do it," took a new turn as the twentieth century came to a close. Sexual practice is no longer only a matter of pleasure or preference. Many today regard sex as the essence of one's personhood. The old sexual revolution of the twentieth century taught everyone to enjoy sex regardless of whether they were married or not. The new sexual revolution of the twenty-first century says that we cannot be truly fulfilled humans without sex. According to Kuehne, "Relationships of obligation have been replaced with relationships of choice, and sexual intercourse has been transformed from being valued primarily for its role in procreation and in cementing a marriage relationship to being a pleasurable and typically essential component of intimate adult romantic relationships."[7]

Instead of being an expression of love, sex *is* love and perhaps even something more. Sex and identity are conflated. Sexual practice isn't just about freedom anymore. These days sex is no longer an appetite or even a practice. Sex is treated as a human right becoming the defining factor in human identity.

———

Sexual desire is pleasurable by nature, but it is also dangerous *because* it is pleasurable and therefore easily misdirected. Sex is dangerous because its effects always stretch beyond the individual. Sex is a public as well as a private concern. Sexual practice affects the community as a whole. "Sex, like any other necessary, precious, and volatile power that is commonly held, is everybody's business," Wendell Berry observes.[8] However, although sex is "everybody's business," it does not automatically follow from this that sex is public property. According to Scripture, our sexual desires are to be gratified within a landscape whose limits have been established by God. This is His right as our Creator. Many treat sex as if it were only a human concern, with limits that can be changed at will or eliminated by majority vote. The Bible paints a very different picture. Sexual desire is a *sacred* pleasure, one that can be enjoyed safely only within the clear boundaries God has established for it.

In a culture whose notions of sex have been shaped by the sexual revolution, talk of boundaries is unpopular. We are more interested in freedom. The changed values of the sexual revolution were enacted under the flag of personal freedom. This is even truer today in the post-sexual revolution era when sexual desire is more than a matter of pleasure. It is now an identity marker. However, when it comes to the Bible's view of human sexuality, there can be no question that real boundaries exist. When the religious leaders asked whether it was lawful for a man to divorce his wife for any reason, Jesus answered in the negative. "Haven't you read," He replied, "that at the beginning the Creator 'made them male and female,' and said, 'For this reason a man will leave his father and mother and be united to his wife, and the two will become one flesh'? So they are no longer two, but one flesh. Therefore what God has joined together, let no one separate" (Matt. 19:5–6). In these verses, Jesus teaches that sex is legitimate only within the marriage context, and marriage is defined by God as the union of male and female. Jesus also warned that the act of adultery has its root in the heart (Matt. 5:28). According to Jesus, those whose sexual desire falls outside the boundaries of God's permission have already committed adultery in their hearts. Our culture has radically redrawn its moral boundaries so that what once was considered lust is now called love, and sexual preference is regarded by many to be malleable. This is more than a minor difference over sexual preference. It amounts to a complete inversion of Christ's intent for sexuality and marriage. What culture used to regard as vice is now virtue. But such a shift involves far more than change in cultural tastes. It is ultimately an inversion of God's idea of what is good. Those things that the Bible defines as vices have become today's dangerous virtues. Not just dangerous but deadly (see Rom. 6:21). Jesus says that our sexual desires are limited by boundaries that God has established.

This is equally true for anything upon which we might set our heart. As sinners, it is not only possible for our desires to move outside those boundaries, but inevitable. When they do, we must deny those desires, no matter what their focus may be. Lust is more than sexual desire, and there is more to love than lust. We are promiscuous in the way we speak of what we love using the term to describe our desires without discriminating between them. Sometimes what we say we love is only a passing fancy. At others, we use the same word to describe something even more basic, merely a bodily response to stimuli. An unmarried couple on a date might declare undying love for one another during dinner and then in the next breath say that they "love" the food that is on their plates. Neither of them thinks this is strange. Afterward, they might decide to "make love," using the same term in a third sense that is more in line with what the Bible calls lust.

Not every affection we feel necessarily qualifies as love, and not all desires are lust in the sinful sense of the word. However, the general tenor of the Bible's teaching about desire is cautionary. Human desire is easily seduced. This note of warning is reflected in the Ten Commandments, which forbids both adultery and coveting in general (Ex. 20:14, 17). The prohibition against adultery implies sexual sin, but in Moses's day, where wives were also categorized as property, it had an economic dimension, too. We can lust for things as well as people and lust may cause us to treat people as things.

The commandment forbidding coveting is broad in its scope. Our neighbor's house, wife, manservant, maidservant, ox, donkey, "or anything that belongs to your neighbor" are all off-limits to our desire. The Hebrew word that is translated "house" in this verse didn't refer to the dwelling so much as those who inhabited it. It might be better translated "household." All of the things mentioned in this verse were marks of personal wealth in the ancient world. It was not wrong to desire or even obtain them, but it is all too easy for our ordinary desires to become illicit.

The dividing line between what is prohibited and what is allowed in this particular commandment has to do with ownership. It is fine to want a spouse or a servant or an ox or donkey. But anything that already belongs to someone else is forbidden. You cannot treat them as your own. You cannot take them by force. Indeed, the language of the commandment is much stronger. You must not even want them. This command strikes at the heart of all the sins associated with the commandments that precede it because it aims at desire itself. Sin always begins with desire (James 1:14–15). Our desires, even the desire for what is ordinary and allowable in other contexts, can make us captives. We find sexual lust the most interesting of the seven sins that the church has traditionally considered to be capital. Sexual lust is the besetting sin of the books, television shows, and movies that entertain us. But desire can be expressed in many different ways and shows up in the other capital sins as well. It is a mistake to dismiss sexual lust as a moral anachronism. But limiting lust to sex is too narrow. Dorothy Sayers notes, "A man may be greedy and selfish; spiteful; cruel, jealous, and unjust; violent and brutal, grasping, unscrupulous, and a liar; stubborn and arrogant; stupid, morose, and dead to every noble instinct—and still we are ready to say of him that he is not an immoral man."[9]

A one-sided view of lust causes the church to send mixed messages regarding lust. Many biblical conservatives are deeply concerned about the normalization of homosexuality. They rightly consider this particular form of immorality to be a threat, not only to the individual's soul but to the future of society as a whole. They do not, however, seem nearly as troubled by heterosexual immorality, which many in their circles have practiced for some time. They emphasize the Bible's explicit condemnation of homosexuality while ignoring its equally explicit condemnation of divorce. Furthermore, the public failure of notable leaders among some of the most conservative churches in other areas of lust, a lust for power, money, and sometimes sex, has exposed not only a lack of self-awareness but an accompanying moral blindness. This has prompted proponents of homosexuality and same-sex marriage to accuse biblical conservatives of hypocrisy, perhaps with good reason.

Others consider homosexual behavior sinful but say that it is no worse than any other sin. Those who take this softer view urge us to stop focusing on the particular sin and instead concentrate on God's loving acceptance. Unfortunately, this supposed grace-oriented approach is often interpreted as a dismissal of sin altogether. If we all lust and every lust is the same, why worry about any of it? Not only does this view ignore the seriousness of sexual sin, but it also minimizes the sin of lust. Neither approach offers practical help to the person who is struggling with lust. They draw the boundaries, either narrowly or broadly, but they do not tell those who are struggling with sexual lust what to do when they find themselves out of bounds.

Ironically, neither does Jesus when he addresses the subject of lust in the Sermon on the Mount. Jesus does not offer four steps for dealing with the problem of lust. Instead of talking about preventive measures, Jesus limits Himself to definition. Jesus' teaching actually intensifies the problem by making it clear that lustful intent is as wrong as the act itself (Matt. 5:28). Jesus' teaching exposes the true boundaries of what constitutes sin in God's eyes and condemns us all. According to Jesus, there is more to sin than the deed. It is possible to avoid the action and yet not escape the sin that prompts the act. Martyn Lloyd-Jones uses a medical analogy to explain Jesus' intent: "Sins are nothing but the symptoms of a disease called sin and it is not the symptoms that matter but the disease, for it is the disease that kills and not the symptoms."[10]

It's important to understand that our struggle with lust is much larger than the desire for sex. In the New Testament, the Greek term that is translated "lust" refers to desire. It can speak of both legitimate and illegitimate desires. In its sinful form, we may fix our desire on many things. It is just as likely to be focused on someone else's possessions or on their success as it is to be an illicit desire for sex. John hints at the full scope of this cardinal sin in 1 John 2:16: "For everything in the world—the lust of the flesh, the lust of the eyes, and the pride of life—comes not from the Father but from the world." As far as John is concerned, when it comes to lust, everything in the world is a potential target. Lust is such a common feature of our culture that it is hard to find a dimension of our experience that is not somehow shaped by it.

Sexual lust is the point of appeal for many of the products that marketers try to sell to us. If lust is not the direct focus of most of the entertainment we consume, it is at least the garnish that its creators use to hold our attention. But this biblical sin has become so commonplace in our culture that it is almost a cliché. Lust's commonplace status does not make it less dangerous to us. If anything, overfamiliarity increases our vulnerability. We have become desensitized and are therefore too tolerant of it, both in our environment and in our own experience. But the biblical sin of lust has many faces, and sometimes its sexual form is only a symptom of something else.

—

In the middle of the last century, Dorothy Sayers observed, "The mournful and medical aspect of twentieth-century pornography and promiscuity strongly suggests that we have reached one of these periods of spiritual depression where people go to bed because they have nothing better to do."[11] According to her diagnosis, in some cases, sexual lust may be a symptom of another of the cardinal sins. It is the one that the ancients used to call acedia or sloth, a condition that sophisticates of another generation once called ennui. Indeed, all these sins are connected. It is a mistake to see them as distinct from one another. All the capital sins and the myriad of expressions of transgression that flow from them all flow from the same root.

But what is opposite of lust? What is the virtue that answers the sin of lust and is its antidote? If the essence of righteousness is to love the Lord your God with all your heart, soul, and mind, and to love your neighbor as yourself, then the essence of sin must be the opposite (Matt. 22:37, 39). To sin is to love yourself at the expense of your neighbor. More than that, it is to love yourself at the expense of God. Sin-shaped love expresses itself primarily in the form of narcissism. It is self-absorbed love. This affection is a distortion of love that, once it has achieved its full effect, actually proves to be an exercise in self-loathing. It is hate masquerading as love, compelling us to engage in self-destructive behavior. Sin promises freedom and delivers slavery. It speaks the language of friendship while treating us like enemies. Sin is a cruel master who promises good wages only to reward our loyalty with hard service, disappointment, and death. For some reason, we return again and again to this false lover and expect a different result.

The answer to sinful lust is love—God's love, which comes to us from the outside, like the righteousness of Christ. Adopting the language that Martin Luther used to speak of Christ's righteousness, we might call it "alien love" because it does not originate with us. It is a love that begins with God and can come to us only as a gift. For the Christian, this greater love is the organizing force for all our other desires. In this regard, love is not so much an emotion as it is a disposition. We might call it a divinely empowered direction for our lives.

Our natural love is limited. The impediment of sin skews our interests in the direction of self. Jesus implies this in the second of the two great commandments, the command to "love your neighbor as yourself" (Matt. 22:39; Mark 12:31, see also Lev. 19:18, 34). We are by nature self-protective and self-interested.

We are able, even in our natural state, to show some concern for others. We may enquire about the health of others when they are sick, or express sympathy when they are grieving. We might even sacrifice ourselves for someone else, offering what Abraham Lincoln called "the last full measure of devotion," if we feel the cause is good enough (Rom. 5:7). But the ability to love others to the same degree that we love ourselves is not natural. Our default orientation is skewed toward our desires. We will easily sacrifice the desires of others on the altar of our self-interest unless something more powerful moves those interests in a different direction.

What is true of lust is true of all the capital sins. Change may require discipline, but it does not begin with discipline. What is required is a miracle of grace. Redirection is necessary if we are to love others in the way that Jesus describes, but there is only one force powerful enough to turn the tide of our desire so that we are as interested in others as we are in ourselves. It is the power of God effected by His love for us. That is why the love that Jesus describes begins not with us but with God. We love others because we love God (1 John 4:21). We love God because God first loved us (1 John 4:10–11, 19).

This may sound too mystical to be practical. Do we merely wait until some divine energy strikes us from the outside and makes us care about those for whom we previously gave no thought? We hear this sort of talk all the time, usually from those who have spent a week or two on some short-term mission trip. "God gave me such a love for the people!" they gush. Perhaps it is true. But it is more likely that they have simply mistaken the excitement of being in strange surroundings or the shock of seeing human need up close for something else. Certainly, they are affected, perhaps even strongly affected. They may feel a sense of pity. But what they are experiencing is the missional equivalent to puppy love. Whether their interest is genuine love can be demonstrated only in the long term after the glow of missional tourism has worn off. Love will prove itself when they learn to cope with all the tedious necessities of living life as strangers in a strange land after they have had full exposure to what seems to be rudeness or arrogance or condescension or outright disinterest.

Fortunately, the analogy of human experience to which Jesus points can help us learn the art of this divine love. God is indeed the source of this love, but it does not operate in some hidden mystical zone. The opportunities to show it and the forms that this love takes are ordinary. The observations of C. S. Lewis are helpful here. "In such a case the Divine Love does not *substitute* itself for the natural—as if we had to throw away our silver to make room for the gold," he explains. "The natural loves are summoned to become modes of Charity while also remaining the natural loves they were."[12] We do not replace our ordinary love with something new that we have never experienced before. Instead, by the grace of God and through the empowerment of His Spirit, we place all our ordinary loves at God's disposal. In this way, His love becomes the love that orders all our other loves. His love is the only love powerful enough to wean us away from our infatuation with ourselves.

With this in mind, the basic rule that Jesus lays when it comes to practicing love is simple to understand: "So in everything, do to others what you would have them do to you, for this sums up the Law and the Prophets" (Matt. 7:12). We do not dismiss our desires but allow them to be our guide by providing a mirror image. What would we want for ourselves, if the circumstances were reversed? Nothing could be simpler. It is the execution that poses the problem for us. We can see it easily enough but we often do not want to live by this rule. The corruption of our sinful nature further complicates matters. Often what we desire from others reflects our sinful self-centeredness, making it an untrustworthy guide for our own behavior. An honest evaluation of Jesus' rule soon reveals that to follow it, we must say no to our desires. We do not need to deny that these desires exist. They are what they are, and Christ already knows that they exist. But we must often deny ourselves. Our mistake has been to believe the lie that we cannot live without the things we desire. This was the original lie that was sold to Eve by Satan. It is the lie that comes with every sinful lust that arises in our hearts.

What Henry Fairlie says of sexual lust is true of all the lesser lusts that captivate us. "Our obsession with our sexuality has led us to develop a wholly false, rather silly, and in the end objectionable view of our natures," he notes. "Our sexual life is taken to be the measure of our entire life."[13] It is not. Neither are the myriad of other desires for which we long. We can live without them. We can live without many of the things we desire most. Indeed, in many cases, we must go without them if we are to live.

The ultimate answer to the false virtue of lust is not better intentions or even willpower. The ultimate remedy is the cross of Jesus Christ. It is only by the cross that we can say no to our sinful desires. This ability is a gift of grace as much as forgiveness. It is the grace of God that "teaches us to say 'No' to ungodliness and worldly passions, and to live self-controlled, upright and godly lives in this present age" (Titus 2:12). The denial is ours, but the power is God's. This capacity to say no to ungodliness is natural only in the sense that it comes from our new nature in Christ: "Those who belong to Christ Jesus have crucified the flesh with its passions and desires" (Gal. 5:24). The Christian does not lose the capacity to lust. Instead, believers gain the ability to deny their sinful desires. These two dimensions exist together and are often a source of great struggle. The old nature (or flesh) "desires what is contrary to the Spirit, and the Spirit what is contrary to the flesh. They are in conflict with each other, so that you are not to do whatever you want" (Gal. 5:17).

What does this mean for our struggle with desire? First, it means that we should not be surprised to find that it is a struggle. The stirring of sinful desire does not mean that the gospel has failed. Neither does it mean that we have no choice but to entertain such desires and act upon them. John Stott notes that the remedy of the cross indicates that we must be pitiless in our denial of the old nature. The cross was reserved for the worst criminals: "If, therefore, we are to 'crucify' our flesh, it is plain that the flesh is not something respectable to be treated with courtesy and deference, but something so evil that it deserves no better fate than to be crucified."[14] In our desire to emphasize God's gracious acceptance of sinners, we may sometimes give the impression that He also tolerates sin. Our desire not to single out any particular type of sin has rehabilitated many that were once regarded as shameful and are now either ignored by the church or treated as acceptable.

Second, the general tone of the New Testament when it speaks of sinful desire is one of hope rather than despair. Although the struggle against lust is lifelong, the Bible not only promises ultimate victory in the life to come but the possibility of overcoming in the present. The stirring of sinful desires is not necessarily the evidence of a spiritual defeat but may be just the opposite. We should treat these stirrings as the death throes of the old nature as it rails against the Spirit. Those who put to death the desires of the sinful nature are simply acting on the assumption that what the Bible says of them is actually true. They recognize that their obligation lies with Holy Spirit who empowers them to say "no" to the flesh (Rom. 8:13; Col. 3:5).

Finally, we should not be so afraid to see our desires go unfulfilled. Countless hours of exposure to marketing has trained us to think that we should have everything we desire. Contemporary teaching about sex implies that we cannot be humans without fulfilling our sexual desires. The truth lies in the opposite direction. Our worst fate may not be that our desires will go unfulfilled but that they will be met. "We are half-hearted creatures, fooling about with drink and sex and ambition when infinite joy is offered us, like an ignorant child who wants to go on making mud pies in a slum because he cannot imagine what is meant by the offer of a holiday at the sea," C. S. Lewis explains. "We are far too easily pleased."[15] This is the problem with human desire. Not that we desire too much, but that we desire too little.

QUESTIONS FOR DISCUSSION:

1. How does sin distort love into lust?

2. Most people identify lust with sexual sin. How else does it manifest itself?

3. Why is biblical love the only real antidote for lust?

CHAPTER 3

Satisfaction:
Coping with the Hunger That Cannot Be Satisfied

I have been bothered by my weight most of my life. As a child, I was heavy, a condition my mother euphemistically described as being "big-boned." I was so obsessed with the fear of being fat that even when I slimmed down in my adolescence, I did not think of myself as thin. I am no longer thin, and I am still bothered. I am not alone. According to some estimates, forty-five million Americans go on a diet each year. In our weight-conscious culture, you would think that we would have a greater sensitivity to the sin the Bible calls gluttony. The truth is most of us wouldn't recognize a glutton if he swallowed us whole. We certainly wouldn't be able to tell whether we are gluttons, and the mirror will not help us. That's because gluttony isn't really about one's weight.

Gluttony is essentially a sin of inordinate appetite. The ancients measured gluttony by the amount of food one consumed. Consequently, the Rule of St. Benedict strictly regulated the number of meals and the amount of food allotted to each monk. Benedict determined that two meals a day were sufficient. Each meal was to include two hot dishes as a concession to individual weakness, "so that the brother who cannot eat one dish may perhaps be able to eat the other."[1] Likewise, Benedict set limits on how much wine should be allowed to each monk. Benedict's standards were lower than the earliest monastic fathers, who tended toward asceticism. "Although we read that wine is never for monks, it is hard to persuade modern monks of this," he admitted. "At least we must all agree that we are not to drink to satiety, but with moderation, 'For wine makes even wise men fall into apostasy.'"[2] The monastic fathers were less pragmatic. They saw food and drink as a major spiritual battleground. "If a king wants to take a city whose citizens are hostile, he first captures the food and water of the inhabitants of that city, and when they are starving subdues them," Abba John the Short observed. "So it is with gluttony. If a man is earnest in fasting and hunger, the enemies which trouble the soul will grow weak."[3] The Christian ascetics viewed hunger as both a virtue and a tool. They seem to have believed that it was better to be hungry than to be full. Like Abba John the Short, they thought that hunger and thirst could be employed to bring all the bodily passions into submission.

Modern proponents of fasting employ similar reasoning. In his book *The Spirit of the Disciplines*, Dallas Willard noted that practicing fasting as a spiritual discipline will teach us an important lesson about ourselves. "It will certainly prove humiliating to us, as it reveals to us how much our peace depends upon the pleasures of eating," he explained. "It may also bring to mind how we are using food pleasure to assuage the discomforts caused in our bodies by faithless and unwise living and attitudes—lack of self-worth, meaningless work, purposeless existence, or lack of rest or exercise."[4] The benefit of fasting as a spiritual discipline is not that it enables one to earn spiritual brownie points, but that it provides a laboratory for experiencing the reality of God's sustaining power. "Fasting confirms our utter dependence upon God by finding in him a source of sustenance beyond food."[5]

Most moderns do not think that the consumption of either food or drink belongs in the category of sin. We are, however, willing to admit that people have psychological problems in these areas. Even Dallas Willard, whose perspective on the subject was informed more by ancient tradition than the modern, blends the psychological with the spiritual. According to the National Association of Anorexia Nervosa and Associated Disorders, approximately thirty million people suffer from eating disorders in the United States.[6] According to the National Institute of Alcohol Abuse and Alcoholism, approximately fifteen million adults over the age of eighteen and an estimated 401,000 adolescents suffer from Alcohol Use Disorder.[7] Calling these behaviors disorders rather than sins and consigning them to the realm of mental health seems to reduce the potential for shame for those who suffer from such problems. It also moves their treatment out of the spiritual dimension, which seems vague and imprecise (if not positively medieval) to moderns, into the more enlightened realm of medicine. We trust our scientists more than our priests and pastors. Nevertheless, most treatment programs for alcohol abuse or eating disorders include a spiritual component, emphasizing the need for help from a "higher power" to overcome addiction.

—

In the twentieth century, the church's perspective on eating changed from the ancient practice of fasting for the spirit to the modern habit of dieting for health. This mirrored a general shift in the culture at large which began in the nineteenth century. "Interest in weight loss as an explicitly religious project began in the mid-twentieth century when neo-evangelicals broke with their fundamentalist forebearers to articulate a new vision for conservative Protestant engagement," historian Lynne Gerber explains. "It was innovative not only for making weight loss a religious imperative but for associating sin not with gluttonous eating habits but with being fat itself."[8] Not only did they consider fat an obstacle to evangelism, but they also viewed it as physical evidence of moral weakness. Although not exclusively one-sided, they especially directed such concerns at women and linked them with sexuality. Christian women were encouraged to work at being slim so they would remain attractive to their husbands. A thin wife was a faithful wife. Not only was a fat wife someone who did not reflect the spiritual fruit of self-control, but she was also a person so selfish that she was willing to jeopardize her marriage.

This view also mirrored the culture at large, especially the culture of the advertising industry, which often sexualizes food. Advertisers invest billions of dollars in their effort to shape popular tastes and influence behavior. Food and alcohol are the primary focus of their campaigns. Women, in particular, are their targets. The resulting message is not only about beauty, but it is also a moral message. Thin isn't just attractive. Thin is good. "In the old days, bad girls got pregnant. These days they get fat—and are more scorned, shamed, and despised than ever before," activist and media critic Jean Kilbourne observes. "Prejudice against fat people, especially against fat women, is one of the few remaining prejudices that is socially acceptable."[9] The climate has changed somewhat since she wrote these words. Models with curves represent what some have called a "body positive" movement. More women are lifting weights, shifting notions of feminine beauty. Yet the message that advertising sends about weight is still mixed. On the one hand, the ideal of beauty it portrays in the majority of cases is still impossible for ordinary people. At the same time, advertising's gospel is one of consumption. "Indulge yourself because you deserve it" the advertisers seem to say. Thin is still the ideal. Women are urged to remain thin to remain attractive to others. But it seems that we can indulge ourselves without fear of consequences. Advertising ignores the inherent contradiction between these two ideals. Advertising regularly targets children, addicts, and those with eating disorders, normalizing self-destructive behavior in its imagery. However, the most dangerous effect of advertising culture may be its subliminal message that we can consume our way to happiness. "Advertising encourages us not only to objectify each other but also to feel that our most significant relationships are with the products that we buy," Kilbourne warns. "It turns lovers into things and things into lovers and encourages us to feel passion for our products rather than our partners."[10]

Body image is sometimes a symbol of moral character in Scripture. Eglon, the king of the Moabites and Israel's enemy, is called "a very fat man" (Judg. 3:17). This descriptive fact set the stage for Ehud's victory gained by plunging his knife deep into the king's belly. But the mention of Eglon's size may also be an implied moral commentary about the king's behavior. He was a wealthy man who had enriched himself at Israel's expense. The Bible notes that Eli, the priest, was "an old man, and he was heavy" to explain the circumstance of his death (1 Sam. 4:18). But this detail is also an allusion to his complicity with his sons fattening themselves on portions of the sacrifices that were not allowed to the priests (see 1 Sam. 2:27–29). Job's friend Eliphaz described the wicked person as someone whose face is covered with fat and whose waist bulges with flesh (Job 15:27). His size symbolizes the prosperity that God will take from him (Job 15:29). When Asaph the psalmist complains that the bodies of the wicked are "healthy and strong" in Psalm 73:4, he actually says that they are "fat." Similarly, the oracle against Ephraim in Isaiah 17:4 warns that the glory of Jacob will fade and the evidence for this is that "the fat of his body will waste away."

Gluttony is not a matter of body size. Gluttony is a sin of consumption. Gluttony is to food what lust is to sex. Gluttony distorts and magnifies bodily appetite until appetite becomes an end in itself. Food, drink, indeed, all our ordinary bodily appetites are part of God's design. But what exactly is His design for our hunger? Functionally, appetite is a means to an end. Proverbs 16:26 says, "The appetite of laborers works for them; their hunger drives them on." This proverb echoes Genesis 3:17–19, where the link between toil and eating is a consequence of sin. But the proverb reveals the complementary benefit that comes from this connection. Hunger is a motivator that drives us to work. We work because we do not want to go hungry (see 2 Thess. 3:10). Hunger also motivates us to take in the sustenance we require for life. But, similar to the curse of Genesis, hunger has two sides. Like work, hunger existed before the fall. As was the case with the first temptation, ordinary hunger can be a gateway to inordinate appetite. Part of the appeal of the forbidden fruit was that it was "good for food" (Gen. 2:9). Sin has the same effect on all our bodily appetites. Hunger can be a motivation, but it can also be a master. Just as sin distorted God's design for work by introducing an element of drudgery into its execution, our hunger can make us slaves.

Slavery to food can take many forms. For some, this bondage expresses itself in a variety of eating disorders. Binge eating, starvation, and binge eating followed by purging are destructive coping methods for dealing with perfectionism and low self-esteem often related to body image. By eating (or not eating), those with eating disorders attempt to heal themselves or make themselves feel better. Food plays an increasingly larger role until it becomes the central focus of life.

For others, bondage to food is reflected in an unhealthy, almost paralyzing, fussiness when it comes to eating. In Paul's day, this was usually a result of misguided religious conviction. In 1 Timothy 4:3, the apostle warns that the last days will be marked by false teachers who demand that their followers live an ascetic lifestyle. They will "forbid people to marry and order them to abstain from certain foods, which God created to be received with thanksgiving by those who believe and who know the truth." Likewise, in Colossians 2:21, he speaks of those whose rule of life was comprised of mainly prohibitive regulations, which he summarizes in the three commands: "Do not handle! Do not taste! Do not touch!"

According to the apostle, a combination of ignorance and pride fueled this bankrupt approach to spirituality. Those who adopted its practices thought that they could obtain eternal life by keeping traditions that focused on "things that are all destined to perish with use" (Col. 2:22). But a habit of putting themselves on display and their tendency to judge anyone who did not follow their rules showed what was really behind it all. Theirs was a show religion marked by false humility and filled with regulations that had "an appearance of wisdom" but were of no real value in "restraining sensual indulgence" (Col. 2:23). Paul was echoing Jesus' teaching in this matter. God's law had labeled certain foods clean and others unclean. Also, the religious leaders of Jesus' day observed traditions, such as ritual washing before the meal, which rendered the act of eating clean or unclean. When some of the Pharisees and teachers of the law criticized His disciples for eating food with "unwashed hands," Jesus countered by saying, "What goes into someone's mouth does not defile them, but what comes out of their mouth, that is what defiles them" (Matt. 15:11). Not only did Jesus reject the tradition of the elders, but His statement also signaled both a sea change in the way God's people approached eating and a correction in the way they understood evil. Evil works from the inside out. It is not eating certain foods which makes one unclean but the thoughts and actions that proceed from the heart. Jesus declared all foods ritually clean (Mark 7:19).

Those who have reservations about eating today are more liable to be driven by a political and social agenda than a religious one, but their spirit is the same, and Paul's directive to the Colossian church equally applies: "Do not let anyone judge you by what you eat or drink" (Col. 2:16). This warning has both a positive and negative sense. Do not let anyone bully you by their personal convictions into a rejection of those things that God has created to be received with thanksgiving. Do not make human traditions the essence of your spirituality. Righteousness is not a matter of one's dietary preferences. The kingdom of God is not a matter of eating and drinking (Rom. 14:17).

In an affluent culture like ours, eating is not just a necessity; it is also a form of recreation. This leads to another type of bondage when it comes to food. Some people are fussy about what they eat because they scorn simple fare. Every meal must be a grand experience. These people view their food the way others look at their possessions. Only the rarest and most expensive will do. Their problem is not that they eat good food but that they view ordinary food, along with those who eat it, with contempt. Their diet is a symptom of greed and pride. They are addicted not to food but to luxury. In the book of Revelation, this is the fare of the great whore of Babylon (Rev. 18:3).

Does this mean that it is a sin to enjoy our food? Are we acting unchristianly if we eat a meal at an expensive restaurant? The Bible teaches that the enjoyment of food is a gift from God. One of the ways God shows His love to the world at large is by supplying us with food. Acts 14:17 says, "Yet he has not left himself without testimony: He has shown kindness by giving you rain from heaven and crops in their seasons; he provides you with plenty of food and fills your hearts with joy." God in His grace has designed eating to be a pleasurable experience. But there are also many good reasons for us to be careful in the way we eat. Food that tastes good is not always good for us or good for the world around us. There are other factors besides taste that inform our eating. One obvious factor is health. Does what I eat or drink strengthen me and contribute to my overall well-being? Or does it work against me and destroy my health?

Another vital question, and one that is often difficult to answer, has to do with the means of production. How has our food been made? Was it safe? Was it ethical? We know nothing about the people or the creatures who have contributed to the meal. Nor are we especially interested in them. We might not enjoy the meal as much if we knew more about what it cost others to provide it for us. "Though I am no means a vegetarian, I dislike the thought that some animal has been made miserable to feed me," Wendell Berry admits. "If I am going to eat meat, I want it to be from an animal that has lived a pleasant, uncrowded life outdoors, on bountiful pasture, with good water nearby and trees for shade."[11] Berry's concern is a biblical one. Proverbs 12:10 says, "The righteous care for the needs of their animals, but the kindest acts of the wicked are cruel." The Mosaic Law included regulations required God's people to care for their animals (Lev. 22:27; Deut. 25:4).

Unfortunately, such concerns can easily lead to another more subtle form of gluttony. It is one that C. S. Lewis characterized as "the gluttony of delicacy." Lewis distinguished the gluttony of delicacy from the gluttony of excess.[12] The gluttony of excess is what we traditionally think of as gluttony. The gluttony of excess is committed by the person who eats for the sake of eating, without regard for taste or even enjoyment. The gluttony of delicacy is the opposite. This form of gluttony involves a self-centered obsession with the nature of what is consumed. Delicate eaters are not just "picky" eaters but are narcissistic eaters. No food is quite good enough. There is no sense of thanksgiving. The food, the host, the server and the others at the table all fade into the background. Another form of this may be those who are obsessive about eating selectively to maintain a certain physique. Such behavior can reflect a kind of body worship with food as the sacrifice. Either way, the belly still dominates.

———

Os Guinness observes that in our day the gluttony of delicacy is more common than traditional gluttony. One reason is that the gluttony of delicacy is a sin of affluence. Our abundance affords us the luxury of being obsessively particular about our food. "The gluttony of delicacy is unquestionably our principal Western problem with food," Guinness observes. "Where food was once simply a matter of human sustenance, enjoyment, and sharing, it is now laden with myriad forms of 'food guilt.'"[13]

As Wendell Berry has observed, however, there are sometimes legitimate reasons for this guilt. The culture of industrial eating has opened the door to many unethical practices. The connection between food production and economics has made the needy also the most vulnerable when it comes to available options. Like the Corinthian church, where those who had the most resources also enjoyed the best food, poor communities are often food deserts. A food desert is an area where people do not have adequate access to healthy foods like fresh fruit, vegetables, and other whole foods. Those who live in these areas are more prone to obesity and diabetes. The food that is available in food deserts tends to be higher priced than in more affluent areas. Those who have the least must pay the most for their food.[14]

We need to strike a balance between what Wendell Berry calls responsible eating and the kind of hypersensitivity that C. S. Lewis labels the gluttony of delicacy. What distinguishes one from the other? I would suggest that it is a combination of information and actionability. Responsible eating requires information and reasonable action. Information will enable me to make ethical decisions about what and how I eat. The action I take needs to be reasonable and achievable. If my concerns lead only to guilt and hand-wringing, I am probably better off following Paul's advice to those who wondered whether they should eat meat sacrificed to idols: "Eat whatever is put before you without raising questions of conscience" (1 Cor. 10:27).

The mistake of gluttony is the error of thinking that appetite is the gateway to satisfaction. In reality, it is the opposite. Hunger by its very nature can never be entirely satisfied. Ecclesiastes 6:7 observes, "Everyone's toil is for their mouth, yet their appetite is never satisfied." Satisfy your hunger with a meal now, and a few hours later that hunger will return. There is nothing to be done about it. When eating becomes an end in itself, it turns into a kind of slavery (1 Cor. 6:12–13). Gluttony conflates desire with satisfaction, expecting more from food than it can supply. The glutton does not eat to live but lives to eat. In reality, our appetites are merely signposts which point to a hunger that cannot be filled by any human means. They point out our emptiness and our need for God. When we look to earthly means to fully and finally satisfy ourselves, we become those whose "god is their stomach" (Phil. 3:19).

Jesus' perspective on eating was personal and practical. Jesus Himself came "eating and drinking" (Matt. 11:19). He taught the church to ask for "daily bread" in the Lord's Prayer (Matt. 6:11). This request that God would satisfy our hunger is the first of the personal petitions that Jesus includes in His prototype prayer. It may seem like this petition shifts the focus of the prayer from heaven to earth, but this is incorrect. The petitions that God's name would be treated as holy and for the coming of the kingdom are just as earthly. If there is a difference, it is in the time frame. The petition for bread is more immediate. In this petition, at least in Matthew's version, Jesus taught His disciples to ask God to give them tomorrow's bread today.

The phrase has puzzled scholars down through the centuries. Exactly what bread does Jesus have in mind? Jerome interpreted the phrase in terms of the kingdom as the bread of the age to come. But Luke's version of this prayer seems to anchor the request in the present (Luke 11:3). According to Luke, we are asking for the bread that we need every day. Even if we accept Jerome's meaning, New Testament scholar Joachim Jeremias is probably right to say that it would be a "crass misunderstanding" to view this as spiritualizing: "For Jesus, there was no opposition between earthly bread and the bread of life, for in the realm of the basileia all earthly things are hallowed."[15]

Ordinary food played an important role in Jesus' ministry just as bread was a central image in His teaching. When Jesus' enemies criticized Him for "eating and drinking," they accused Him of being "a glutton and a drunkard, a friend of tax collectors and sinners" (Matt. 11:19; Luke 7:34). The complaint, raised by the religious leaders who followed the scrupulous dietary regulations of Mosaic law and Jewish custom, may shed some light what they thought gluttony looked like. It's not that Jesus was eating too much. He was eating too many meals with the wrong sort of people. Jesus aggravated matters further by ignoring some of the customs related to eating that the rabbis had added to the requirement of the Mosaic Law (Matt. 15:2).

The connection between food and Jesus' ministry should not surprise us. He lived in a culture in which worship and eating were connected. Jesus made communal eating a part of the sacred life of the church when at the last Passover meal He ate with the disciples, He shifted the focus of the meal to His suffering and commanding His disciples to eat the meal together after His departure (Luke 22:19; 1 Cor. 11:24–26). In this way, the

Lord's Supper entered the life of the church. "The first Christians remembered not just the last but many meals of Jesus as models for their own eating," Andrew McGowan notes. "Those meals also belonged to a wider cultural tradition of shared eating and drinking, within which the emerging eucharistic meal tradition took its place and claimed its significance."[16] Jesus' directive that His disciples should pray for daily bread in Matthew 6:11 assumes a basic truth. We must eat to live. If we do not eat, we die. Some foods may be a luxury, but eating is not. Jesus also told His disciples not to be anxious about what they would eat or drink (Matt. 6:25). Jesus did not believe such things were trivial, but the opposite. The pagans run after such things but not the children of God because "your heavenly Father knows that you need them" (Matt. 6:32). As an infant Jesus was nourished at His mother's breast. As a child His earthly parents provided for Him. Jesus learned a trade and worked for a living until He began His public ministry (Mark 6:3). During His ministry the group of women who followed Him "cared for his needs" (Mark 15:41; Luke 8:1–3). Jesus knew from personal experience what it meant to need daily bread.

At the same time, Jesus taught that life is more than food (Luke 12:23). Food is necessary for life but is not itself life. We do not live by bread alone (Matt. 4:4). Life is more than food just as the body is more than clothing. Food is necessary for life but is not synonymous with life. The power of Jesus' teaching on this matter is grounded in His assumption that food is needful. We need to eat, but when we conflate life with the means we rely upon to sustain that life we set the table for idolatry. It does not have to be food. We can rely upon our health or finances or even clothing. Like the Israelites who worshiped the bronze serpent that Moses held up in the wilderness, we forget that our life does not come from the things that God uses to sustain it (2 Kings 18:4).

—

Like all the capital sins, gluttony usually travels in company. The Bible links the sin of gluttony with other capital sins like greed and sloth. Proverbs 23:21 warns that "drunkards and gluttons become poor, and drowsiness clothes them in rags." Gluttony is often a collective sin. In Proverbs 23:21, the writer suggests that gluttony is contagious. People fall into this sin by associating with those who "drink too much wine or gorge themselves on meat" (Prov. 23:20). Gluttony is also a cultural sin (Titus 1:12). Even when it is committed in a communal context, the self-centered focus of gluttony isolates the glutton from everyone else who shares in the meal. When some in the Corinthian church distorted the eucharistic meal by refusing to wait for others, they were observing the Lord's Supper with a gluttonous spirit (1 Cor. 11:21).

Paul's complaint may seem strange to us. Our communion celebrations usually involve only a thimble-sized portion of juice and a small wafer or bit of bread. In the Corinthian church, communion was celebrated with an actual meal. Although its primary purpose was to celebrate our participation in the body and blood of Christ and thereby "proclaim the Lord's death until He comes," a secondary aim of the meal seems to have been to provide food for the poor in the church. The thanksgiving prayer that concluded the eucharistic celebration prescribed in the ancient handbook of church order known as the *Didache*, and which reflects traditions that may go back as far as the first century, was recited "after you have had enough" (*Didache* 10:1).

Eating is always a communal activity, even when we dine alone because food is the product of the community. For most of us, the food we eat is usually not produced by us. Others grow the grain and tend the animals that make up our meal. All of this, in turn, comes from the hand of the Creator "who supplies seed to the sower and bread for food" (2 Cor. 9:10). The way we get and consume our food and drink hides this fact. As Wendell Berry has wryly observed, "The passive American consumer, sitting down to a meal of pre-prepared or fast food, confronts a platter covered with inert, anonymous substances that have been processed, dyed, breaded, sauced, gravied, ground, pulped, strained, blended, prettified, and sanitized beyond resemblance to any part of any creature that ever lived."[17] Instead of seeing eating as both a community and a communal act, we have become what Berry calls "industrial" eaters. "The products of nature and agriculture have been made, to all appearances, the products of industry," Berry explains. "And the result is a kind of solitude, unprecedented in human experience, in which the eater may think of eating as, first, a purely commercial transaction between him and a supplier and then as a purely appetitive transaction between him and his food."[18]

Eating is a commercial transaction, but it is much more than this. Eating is a spiritual activity. God used food to teach Israel to trust Him during their sojourn in the wilderness. Moses described their experience in these words, "He humbled you, causing you to hunger and then feeding you with manna, which neither you nor your ancestors had known, to teach you that man does not live on bread alone but on every word that comes from the mouth of the LORD" (Deut. 8:3). Israel's journey through the wilderness was a laboratory experience of God's provision. The experience taught them that even though God sometimes withholds our desires, He also provides what we need. Sometimes what God provides comes in the form of simple fare. Manna in the wilderness was miraculous food, but it was not luxurious. Numbers 11 describes how the children of Israel grew weary of it. They complained that the menu never varied. "We remember the fish we ate in Egypt at no cost—also the cucumbers, melons, leeks, onions and garlic," they said. "But now we have lost our appetite; we never see anything but this manna!"

Their complaint highlights an often unrecognized feature of the sin of gluttony. Gluttony is not always about the amount of food that one consumes. It is ultimately a matter of dissatisfaction with God's provision. Israel's criticism was much more than a complaint about taste or menu. Ultimately, it was a rejection of God Himself (Num. 11:20). This is the heart of the sin of gluttony.

Jesus quoted Deuteronomy 8:3 when Satan challenged Him to prove His deity by turning stones into bread. Satan came to Him and said, "If you are the Son of God, tell these stones to become bread" (Matt. 4:3). The crux of Satan's challenge focused on Jesus' identity as much as His hunger. The conditional "if" really has the force of "since." Since Jesus is the Son of God, He should command the stones to become bread. It is an appeal to privilege. Why should Jesus, of all people, have to go hungry? In a way, this was just a variation on the original temptation in the Garden. Satan asked, "Did God really say, 'You must not eat from any tree in the garden'?" (Gen. 3:1). Satan cast doubt on God's motive for withholding the fruit of the tree of the knowledge of good and evil from Adam and Eve. We are afraid of emptiness. We do not believe that God should withhold any desire from us. When our desires go unmet, we question God's goodness.

———

How then do we deal with gluttony? The primary method the Bible prescribes is self-denial. "When you sit to dine with a ruler, note well what is before you, and put a knife to your throat if you are given to gluttony," the writer of Proverbs warns. "Do not crave his delicacies, for that food is deceptive" (Prov. 23:1–3). The hyperbolic language of the proverb is intended to drive home a simple point. Every desire we have does not need to be met. Every appetite need not be satisfied. Every thirst does not need to be slaked. We can live happy and fulfilled lives without getting everything that we desire.

The power to say no to desire begins with the will, but it requires more than willpower. In the Christian life, self-denial is a work of grace. Titus 2:11–14 says that God's grace, "teaches us to say 'No' to ungodliness and worldly passions, and to live self-controlled, upright and godly lives in this present age, while we wait for the blessed hope—the appearing of the glory of our great God and Savior, Jesus Christ, who gave himself for us to redeem us from all wickedness and to purify for himself a people that are his very own, eager to do what is good."

Self-denial is not an end in itself. By practicing self-denial, we discover how God supplies all we truly need. One way that God's people have learned this truth is by practicing the discipline of fasting. "Fasting confirms our utter dependence upon God by finding in him a source of sustenance beyond food," Dallas Willard explains. "Through it, we learn by experience that God's word to us is a life substance, that it is not food ('bread') alone that gives life, but also the words that proceed from the mouth of God (Matt. 4:4)."[19] Willard points out that the reason for doing this is not because eating is bad. Nor is fasting our normal way of life. "In the disciplines of abstinence, we abstain to some degree and for some time from the satisfaction of what we generally regard as normal and legitimate desires."[20] Saying no to these things teaches us that we *can* say no to them. Fasting reminds us of our dependence upon God and provides a context where we can experience His sustaining power.

Fasting will also show us how large a role food plays in our lives. Few of us eat to live. We eat for comfort. We eat out of boredom. We eat to avoid unwelcome tasks. We eat to make ourselves feel better about ourselves. We eat for the high that it gives us. Oddly enough, we no longer eat to experience community. We do not eat with a sense of God's presence. Wendell Berry is right when he says, "Our kitchens and other eating places more and more resemble filling stations, as our homes more and more resemble hotels."[21] He might have added that our churches more and more resemble fast-food restaurants. What we call fellowship is little more than small talk about sports and the weather over coffee and doughnuts while the church's most sacred "meal" is only a bit of bread and drop of juice that we dash off while looking at the clock.

For this reason, another remedy for gluttony is not abstinence but healthy eating. Just as we discipline ourselves to ignore our appetite, we must practice the discipline of eating responsibly. Some of the habits that come with this discipline are disarmingly ordinary. Begin by following the custom of Christ and the apostles by acknowledging God's presence as the host and provider of the meal. Begin each meal with thanksgiving (Matt. 14:19; Acts 27:35). View each meal as an opportunity for communion as well as an occasion for eating. If others are present, slow down long enough to engage them in meaningful conversation. Learn to appreciate the larger community that has contributed to the meal by giving some thought to the chain of supply. How many people have participated in its preparation from farm to table? What did it take to bring the food to your plate? To whom and how best can you express your thanks?

The kingdom of God is not a matter of eating and drinking, but food is an important part of our earthly life. Eating has played a vital role in the worship as well as the ordinary fellowship of the church, and it will continue to be part of our experience in the life to come. As important as food is, it was never meant to be an end in itself. Gluttony elevates our expectation so that we end up seeking a degree of satisfaction from our eating that it was never meant to provide. Gluttony is more than an emphasis on the pleasure of eating. It involves an exageration of that pleasure. Gluttony, like greed, is also a sin of excess. Because our eating is bound up with our economics, gluttony is an act of social injustice as well as the misuse of our appetite. Those who have the most resources have access to the best food. Food deserts, where residents don't have access to a food source, are usually located in low income communties. The result is far more serious than a difference in menu options. It leads to a difference in health, overall quality of life, and even life expectancy. Not only has gluttony been accepted in our private eating. We have accepted it as a social condition in the population at large.

Few things are as common to everyday life as eating. Few things are as essential to our life as food. Jesus recognized this fact and taught the church to pray for daily bread. The basic rule when it comes to our eating is the same rule that guides us in all of life: "So whether you eat or drink or whatever you do, do it all for the glory of God" (1 Cor. 10:31).

QUESTIONS FOR DISCUSSION:

1. Do you think our weight-conscious culture makes us more or less prone to gluttony?

2. Why is gluttony more about unfulfilled desire than about eating?

3. Do you think there is a relationship between gluttony and today's culture of marketing? Why or why not?

CHAPTER 4

Prosperity:
Why Wanting More Means We Will Never Have Enough

A while back, I noticed a menu option on my retirement account's website labeled "net worth." When I clicked on it, the site asked me to type in information about my assets and liabilities. The result was a brightly colored graph that represented the total of all my worldly goods. I have looked at it many times since then, and its effect is always the same. Instead of making me feel secure about my future, it leaves me anxious. No matter how much I have, it seems that I would like to have just a little more. The experience reminds me of a conversation an electrician I know once had with a wealthy man whose home he had rewired. "So how much money is enough?" the electrician wanted to know. The rich homeowner smiled and replied, "Just a little more!"

There is a word for this condition. It is what the Bible calls greed. Greed, like lust and gluttony, is a sin of appetite. While lust is usually associated with sex, and gluttony is linked with food, greed is a similar inordinate desire for money and possessions. Most of us are pretty sure we don't suffer from greed because we don't see ourselves as wealthy. The rich are greedy, perhaps, but not us. The flaw in this reasoning is that desiring is not necessarily synonymous with having. It is certainly possible for a rich person to be greedy, but so might one who is poor. It is not the having but the wanting that is the problem. The adjective that best expresses the impulse of greed is not "most" but "more." Whatever I possess will not be enough if I succumb to the influence of greed. I must always have a little more.

Wanting is not the only symptom of greed. Having can be just as much of a stumbling block. In Luke 12:13–21, Jesus told a parable about a wealthy farmer whose ground produced a good crop. The farmer had been so successful that he had run out of room. After giving the matter thought, the farmer decided to renovate. He planned to tear down his old barns and replace them with bigger ones that would hold his grain and his possessions. To most of us, this seems like a good plan. It is the sort of thing we would do. If the legion of home improvement shows on cable television are any indication, it is the kind of thing that we do all the time. It only makes sense. The conversation the man has with himself sounds a lot like the sales pitch I read on my retirement website. "Then he said, 'This is what I'll do. I will tear down my barns and build bigger ones, and there I will store my surplus grain. And I'll say to myself, 'You have plenty of grain laid up for many years. Take life easy; eat, drink and be merry'" (Luke 12:18–19).

But what most of us would consider a parable about the need for wise money management and planning (the sort of thing we see in commercials for investment firms every day) turns out to be a tragic comedy. Even as the man congratulates himself, God engages him in a different kind of conversation: "But God said to him, 'You fool! This very night your life will be demanded from you. Then who will get what you have prepared for yourself?'" (Luke 12:20).

On the surface, this little story is too easy. It is almost a cliché. We can immediately recognize the villain of the story. That is until we read the question that prompted Jesus to tell the parable in the first place. Someone in the crowd came to Jesus with a demand: "Teacher, tell my brother to divide the inheritance with me" (Luke 12:13). Is this a case of greed or is it an appeal for justice? The nature of the request suggests that it was made by the younger of the two brothers. By law, he was entitled to a 1/3 share of his father's inheritance (Deut. 21:17). This alone would be enough to make most of us bristle. Most of us would feel we were entitled to an equal share, no matter what the law said.

But Jesus did not even seem interested in protecting his legal rights in this matter. Jesus replied, "'Man, who appointed me a judge or an arbiter between you?' Then he said to them, 'Watch out! Be on your guard against all kinds of greed; life does not consist in an abundance of possessions'" (Luke 12:14–15). There are two parts to Jesus' surprising response. One is an assessment of this man's false view of Jesus. The other is an implied evaluation of the man's motive in making the request. The man was merely trying to use Jesus to get what he wanted. There was no devotion reflected in his brusque demand. He speaks to Jesus as if He were merely a legal functionary. There are plenty of others who can act as judge and referee such disputes. The man's whole approach to Jesus is demanding and self-interested. More importantly, the one who knew what was in the hearts of all people had diagnosed this man's true condition. Despite any legal standing he may have had, the root motive behind his demand was one of greed.

Both the man's request and the scenario described in Jesus' parable reveal a sobering fact about greed. It often comes to us dressed in respectable clothes. For the man who made the request, greed clothed itself in the guise of justice. He believed that he was only looking for an equitable distribution of the family's wealth. For the rich man in Jesus' parable, greed disguised itself as practicality. He had to do something with all the grain his fields had produced. He couldn't just leave them to rot. Besides, there was the future to consider. It was only reasonable that he should provide for himself. The rich man's flaw was not his plan but his perspective toward the things he owned. He had failed to include God in His net worth. "This is how it will be with whoever stores up things for themselves but is not rich toward God," Jesus explained after telling the parable (Luke 12:21). The man who made the request that prompted the parable was guilty of a similar error. "Watch out! Be on your guard against all kinds of greed; life does not consist in an abundance of possessions," Jesus warned His disciples upon hearing the man's demand (Luke 12:15). Greed will make atheists of us in the end. Like gluttony, we expect greed to give us something that it cannot provide. Just as gluttony leaves us hungering and thirsting, greed will lead us to poverty no matter how many possessions we acquire.

—

In 2011, the Occupy Wall Street movement spawned a series of protests in New York and other major cities aimed at drawing public attention to economic inequality. Those who participated would agree that greed is a problem but would probably not consider it to be their problem. One of the ways we have rehabilitated greed is by limiting it to a narrow band within the larger population (the rich) and explaining away our own struggle with greed as merely a desire for prosperity. Churches that used to teach classes on only the Bible now also teach courses in money management. Of course, the Bible does have something to say about money. But what it says is often cautionary. Is it possible that what we call financial freedom and wisdom might be greed in disguise?

Perhaps the great difficulty we face in this matter is the fact that none of us sees ourselves as greedy. We are as oblivious as the man in Jesus' parable. We are pretty sure we can spot greed in others. There are some people who, as far as we are concerned, have more than their share. But we do not fall into that category. We are, for the most part, people of modest means. If we have a little more than we thought we would, it is because we worked hard, saved, and have been wise in our financial dealings. Or maybe we are like the majority of those first heard Jesus' parable. We have limited means. Jesus believed that the poor needed to be warned about the danger of greed as much as the rich. We might be outraged by this if it weren't for the fact that Jesus Himself was one of the poor. He had no place to lay His head (Matt. 8:20). Jesus was dependent upon the generosity of others for His support. At the time of His death, Jesus owned only the clothes on His back (see John 19:24).

Greed is a problem for the rich, the working class, the middle class, and the poor because greed does not focus on what we have but what we want. Greed substitutes things for God. In this respect, greed is a form of idolatry (Col. 3:5). According to Jesus, greed is a misconstrual of life itself. It persuades us that life consists of piling up of goods. If we have enough, we will live. How much is enough? It does not matter how much or how little we possess. As the rich man observed to my friend, "Just a little more!"

Jesus' warning also reveals that greed comes in many forms. "Watch out!" He says. "Be on your guard against all kinds of greed." One of the ways we drop our guard is by defining greed too narrowly. We associate greed with a particular income level or specific set of goods. Somehow the very specific picture we have of the greedy person never looks like us. The forms that greed can take are so various that we could devote an entire book to them and still not exhaust the subject. But the Bible does single out a few of the most common modes that greed assumes. One of its most basic forms is the greed of desire.

The old-fashioned term used for this kind of greed is covetousness. This mode of greed is singled out in the Ten Commandments (Ex. 20:17; Deut. 5:21). Desire is the fundamental characteristic of covetousness, but it is a particular kind of desire. The problem with covetousness is not that we want the same kind of thing that a neighbor has. If my neighbor buys a particular kind of car and I decide to buy the same make and model, I am not necessarily acting out of covetousness. I may simply agree with my neighbor's choice. The distinguishing mark of covetousness according to the commandment is the fact that I want something that belongs to someone else. It is not that I want a car or property or a spouse *like* theirs. I want *their* car. I want *their* property. I want *their* spouse. There is more at stake than the thing itself. The trouble with covetousness is that the thing I desire is all I have in view. I am so focused on what is my neighbor's that I have lost sight of my neighbor altogether.

The intent of God's commandment goes beyond the prohibition. Not only am I to respect others' right of ownership, but I also need to protect it as well. The commandment forces me to look beyond my own interests and to look after the best interests of my neighbor as well (see Phil. 2:4). Once again we are confronted with the isolating nature of sin. Covetousness reduces my world to a population of one so that the only desires I can see are my own. I live in a world of desire, and all I see around me are objects of desire. Other people do not matter. Even God does not matter. The only relationship (if you can call it that) that matters is the one I hope to have with the thing I want.

Although the commandment dealing with covetousness focuses primarily on tangible objects like my neighbor's house, land, ox, or donkey, what I covet does not necessarily have to be material. I may covet their job or their popularity. I may covet the esteem granted to them by others and want it for myself. This is more than a simple desire for the same kind of job or a desire to be well thought of by others. Beneath covetousness is a wish to deprive. I want what is theirs.

Related to covetousness is another mode of greed that we might describe as the greed of accumulation. We used to call this hoarding. Hoarding can be a psychological disorder where people find it difficult to discard things. People with a hoarding disorder often live in clutter and obtain things for which they have no real use. In many cases, a hoarding disorder is merely an inconvenience, but it can also be detrimental to one's quality of life. The kind of hoarding that the Bible condemns is different and involves the hoarding of wealth. James 5:3 warns of the judgment reserved for those who have "hoarded wealth in the last days." The context indicates that this is more than a blanket condemnation of the rich. The condemnation targets those who enrich themselves by withholding the wages due to those who have worked for them. These hoarders not only are wealthy, but also have "lived on earth in luxury and self-indulgence" (James 5:4). James echoes the picture Jesus paints in the parable of the rich fool. Those he condemns pile up goods for themselves without regard for God or for the larger responsibilities that come with the wealth that God has provided. Such criticism will seem excessive to many moderns. We no longer consider greed to be a vice. While an old idiom spoke of "an embarassment of riches," today's consumers have been taught to be proud of luxury and self-indulgence.

Wealth is a blessing, but it comes with the responsibility of stewardship. We work to provide for our own needs and those of our family (1 Tim. 5:8). We also work so that we may have something to share with those who are in need (Eph. 4:28). This responsibility is scaled according to ability. Those who have more can give more. Giving is based on what we have (1 Cor. 16:2; 2 Cor. 8:11–12). Giving is also an act of grace (2 Cor. 8:6). God's grace enables those who have to give voluntarily and without reluctance (2 Cor. 9:7). If giving is a duty, it is one that is to be fulfilled freely and not under compulsion. There is no prescribed formula for how much we give other than that it should be according to our means. The biblical standard is that our giving should be in keeping with our income. God's generosity to us is the source of our generosity to others.

Wealth, like poverty, comes with its own peculiar temptations. "Keep falsehood and lies far from me; give me neither poverty nor riches, but give me only my daily bread," Proverbs 30:8–9 petitions. "Otherwise, I may have too much and disown you and say, 'Who is the LORD?' Or I may become poor and steal, and so dishonor the name of my God." Either extreme can compromise our faith. Each can forget God. "Wealth is particularly insidious in giving its bearers the illusion of independence, separateness, and 'being in control,'" Stanley Hauerwas observes. "But all of us in one way or another willingly submit to the illusion that we can rid our world of chance and surprise."[1]

This was the fantasy of the rich fool in Jesus' parable. He hoped to accumulate enough goods to guarantee his future. It was not the rich man's failure to take death into account that made him a fool but his inability to know his life's breadth (Luke 12:20). The rich fool took too much for granted. He assumed that his life span would last for "many years," when in reality he had but a few hours remaining. If we cannot control or forestall the hour of our death, how can we hope to guarantee our future simply by piling up goods?

The language God uses when He confronts the rich fool implies that the man's life does not belong to him: "This very night your life will be demanded from you" (Luke 12:20). This rebuke explodes the rich man's illusion of control. It also implies that an accounting is about to take place. The debt is about to be called in. His life and his wealth were not for his benefit alone. This is one of the reasons the Bible condemns hoarding. Hoarding keeps us from acting as conduits of God's blessing to others. Those who hoard claim ownership of what ultimately belongs to God.

Perhaps the most common mode of greed could be characterized as the greed of anxiety. Anxiety about the future drove the rich fool in Jesus' parable to hoard. But we do not necessarily have to be rich to fall into this kind of greed. Jesus described this mode of greed in the Sermon on the Mount when He warned His disciples not to worry about what they would eat, drink, or wear (Matt. 6:25). It is a mistake to think of greed as the exclusive sin of the rich. Greed is not only a sin of excess. It is just as easy to focus our greed on necessities.

When Jesus addresses the problem of greed in the Sermon on the Mount, He points to a weakness on two fronts. One side is the weakness of the things that are the objects of our greed. The other is a weakness within ourselves. We lean too heavily on the things we accumulate by depending on them rather than on God. Things are too undependable. Something as fragile as a moth can ruin them. Their condition deteriorates. A thief may steal them (Matt. 6:19).

One reason we worry so easily is because we know instinctively that our position is fragile. We genuinely need the things that Jesus tells us not to worry about (Matt. 6:25). Food and clothing are not luxuries. Yet experience proves that we cannot rely upon such things. Our clothes wear out, or we grow out of them. The meal we have eaten today will not sustain us tomorrow. We have good reason to be concerned about such things. When you take possession of your shiny new car, its value decreases as soon as you drive it off the lot. It only takes the breath of a rumor to send the amount that gave you so much comfort when you calculated your net worth this morning into a steep decline.

Jesus acknowledges our vulnerability. He does not want us to be distracted by such fears. The rich are not the only ones who are in danger of slipping into the idolatry that is greed. This particular form of idolatry is as much a matter of misplaced faith as it is a matter of accumulation. Our anxiety is an indication that we have shifted our confidence from the God who provides for our needs to the things that we need. We have confused the means that God uses to sustain our life with the source of that life. In His teaching on this subject, Jesus redirects our attention so that it is no longer divided. He does not dismiss our need but points us to the care of our heavenly Father (Matt. 6:25).

—

Greed, like gluttony, is a cultural sin. Today's culture has redefined greed. We call it prosperity and consider it to be a virtue. According to Dorothy Sayers, the character of this sin has changed with the times. "It was left for the present age to endow covetousness with glamor on a big scale and to give it a title that it could carry like a flag," Sayers explains. "It occurred to somebody to call it enterprise. From the moment of that happy inspiration, covetousness has gone forward and never looked back. It has become a swaggering, swashbuckling, piratical sin, going about with its hat cocked over its eye, and with pistols tucked into the tops of its jack-boots."[2] Sayers notes that earlier generations felt differently about greed. They were embarassed by it. Greed was a cause for shame. The modern age rehabilitated greed and gave it a new name. Now we call it enterprise. Or in some cases, especially in certain church circles, greed has been spiritualized and christened as "prosperity."

In our day, the ability to store up treasure is considered a benchmark of success. Yet in Matthew 6:19, Jesus warns, "Do not store up for yourselves treasures on earth, where moths and vermin destroy, and where thieves break in and steal." Frugality is a virtue. Greed is a vice. It is not wrong to save or provide for ourselves and our families. Yet our possessions are not meant to have our heart (Matt. 6:19–21). The heart belongs to God.

We defer to the opinion of those who have obtained much, not because they are necessarily wise or godly, but simply because they have much. The wealthy control the seats of power in public office and our churches. This is not a new pattern. The New Testament letter of James makes it clear that this has been a temptation to the church from its inception (James 2:2–6). It is certainly not wrong for the wealthy to be a part of the church nor is it a sin for someone who is rich to be highly regarded or function as a leader. It is wrong for the church to show deference to the rich simply because they are rich. This is a reflection of the church's own greed and its tendency to depend on large donors more than upon God. "Just as gluttony thrives on our little greeds, so the sin of covetousness thrives on our little acts of avarice–on the stupid and irresponsible shareholder, for example, who is out to get money for nothing," Dorothy Sayers observes.[3]

If lust is the primary garnish of our regular entertainment, greed holds second place. How many of the so-called reality television and games shows we watch use greed as the carrot that motivates their contestants to go to extreme measures or put themselves on embarrassing display? This is why reality television is so popular. "Virtually all of reality TV from *Keeping Up With the Kardashians* to all the house rehab shows are materialistic porn," a colleague of mine recently observed. "They're portraying greed and calling it good." Calling all these shows materialistic porn my be extreme. Yet many television programs appeal to our fascination with—and perhaps our jealousy of— the lifestyles of the rich and famous. The lure of greed shapes public policy and economic planning in our states and cities. School funding is increasingly dependent upon the promise of income from lottery sales, an enterprise that is built mostly upon the backs of the poor. The poorest third of Americans buy more than half of all lottery tickets.[4] States hoping for a tax windfall are rushing to legalize recreational marijuana use despite warnings from the medical community that the drug's detrimental effects are liable to outweigh its benefits.[5]

One of the symptoms of this collective greed is our national habit of justifying unwise practices like these based on some perceived monetary value. We enable the exploitation of others or ignore the negative effects of public policies because they will be good for the economy. Economics has become the primary, if not the only, ethical filter that modern society employs when shaping public policy. This is a kind of economic utilitarianism, where the well-being of the few is sacrificed for the good of the many on the altar of economic improvement. In actual practice it often seems that the opposite happens. A few reap the profits while the many are harmed.

One reason for this is because we think of greed only in terms of what is acquired. Just as gluttony is often identified only with the volume of food consumed, we tend to measure greed by the number of possessions one accumulates. We do not think of the larger questions that are also associated with greed. We do not see the larger picture, which not only involves the acquisition of goods but the means we use to obtain them. To truly address the problem of greed, we must expand our focus to things like the proper place of work in human life and the nature of good work. What are an employer's obligations to those they employ and what sort of effort is due to the employer? What role does the community have in all of this? Like all the capital sins, greed does not work in isolation. It cooperates with other sins like sloth, envy, and pride.

We legitimize greed when we redefine it as prosperity. Since greed is bad and prosperity is good, we convince ourselves that there is nothing unhealthy about the constant desire for more. The Bible does indeed speak well of prosperity. In the Old Testament, the prosperity of the patriarchs was attributed to God's blessing (Gen. 32:9, 12; 39:2).

God provides prosperity (3 John 2). Our giving springs from His generosity to us (1 Cor. 16:2). But what is good can also be turned against us. Indeed, one way to understand the nature of any sin is to see it as a distortion of the good that God has provided. Our mistake is not that we seek prosperity but that we have so narrowly defined what we mean by the term.

Prosperity has an economic component, especially in the Old Testament. The prosperity of the biblical patriarchs was marked by an increase in flocks and servants (Gen. 30:43). The promise of prosperity to Israel included children, livestock, and crops (Deut. 28:11). Prosperity includes sufficiency in one's means of support but it is not limited to this. These concrete symbols of prosperity also imply a certain quality of life: "In that day each of you will invite your neighbor to sit under your vine and fig tree,' declares the LORD Almighty" (Zech. 3:10; cf. Micah 4:4). The prophets make clear that the ultimate fulfillment of these promises will take place in the kingdom of God.

These images of children, livestock, and crops are symbols of the prosperity God promises and are not its essence. The problem with greed is that it confuses the symbols with the thing they represent. If we make the symbols our ultimate goal, we will inevitably fall short of the reality. The symbols cannot substitute for the kingdom itself. "By cleverness, energy, and diligence one can acquire a good many of the goods which are generally considered adjuncts of the happy life: food and drink, house, garden, books, a rich and beautiful wife (perhaps)" theologian Josef Pieper notes. "But we cannot make all these acquisitions, or even a single one of them, quench that thirst so mysterious to ourselves for what we call 'happiness.'"[6]

The earthly symbols of prosperity provide a framework for understanding the promise of the kingdom that is coming. They employ the language of human experience depicting eternal blessings in earthly terms and enabling us to see that there is some continuity between the life we live now and the life to come. Jesus does something similar when He describes the blessedness of the kingdom in the Beatitudes. But there is a shocking inversion when it comes to Jesus' picture of who experiences these blessings. They do not come to the well-heeled and successful of the world. It is not the go-getters or the ambitious that obtain the blessing. Instead Jesus promises it to the poor, the meek, and the hungry (Matt. 5:3–12).

Christians and non-Christians alike have taken comfort from the Beatitudes. But this is largely because they have missed the point. Jesus' teaching had the opposite effect upon His original hearers. When He finished with the Sermon on the Mount, His audience was "amazed" by what He had said (Matt. 7:28). The portrait of the kingdom He had painted for them upended the values they had been taught all their lives. It suggested that they were in pursuit of the wrong things. Even worse, Jesus' teaching implied that the means and the methods they assumed would eventually deliver blessedness into their hands was working against them. "We should not think that Jesus merely wanted to give us a few maxims of practical wisdom, that he merely intended to talk about the blessing of suffering and poverty and console us by telling us that suffering would make us more mature," Helmut Thielicke warns. "Jesus knew all too well that it can turn out just the opposite, that a man can break down under suffering, that it can drive us into cursing instead of prayer, and that its ultimate effect will perhaps be bitter complaining and accusing of God for his injustice."[7] But this is exactly what we do when it comes to Jesus' teaching in the Beatitudes. We leach all the mystery of the kingdom from it until all we have left is an insipid form of folk wisdom. We infuse Jesus' message with sentimentalism, diluting it until it is little more than a Hallmark sentiment. Good things come to those who wait. The sun will come up tomorrow. Do your best.

In the Beatitudes, Jesus deconstructs our notion of what prosperity looks like, speaking of it under the rubrics of blessing and kingdom. The strange blessings of the kingdom seem to indicate that it is not acquisition that paves the way to true prosperity but loss. We should not confuse Jesus' message with the kind of sentimental drivel modern Christians so often spout about poverty and hunger. I am thinking of the sort of statements one sometimes hears from people who have returned home from short-term mission trips to some poverty-stricken country. "Yes they are poor, but they have so much," someone gushes. "They are so simple and genuine." These sorts of observations are a kind of inversion designed to ease the conscience of those who are returning to more prosperous circumstances by implying that the poor are the ones who are better off. We are beset by materialism while they are not. We are distracted and busy, but the poor live a carefree lifestyle. This sort of thinking is the modern economic equivalent to the nineteenth-century myth of the happy slave. Such thinking is a result of superficial exposure to the hard realities of economic deprivation. The Bible is sympathetic to the poor, but it never sentimentalizes poverty.

If Jesus isn't sentimentalizing poverty, hunger, loss, and persecution in the Beatitudes, what is He doing? He is revealing the key to prosperity by showing us what the life of the kingdom looks like. The Beatitudes are not a path to prosperity. They are the shape of it. We do not obtain prosperity by treating the Beatitudes like a set of rules. The Beatitudes show us what this prosperity looks like once it is in our possession. Prosperity is the kingdom, and the kingdom is Christ. Jesus shows us that there is a kind of addition that comes to those who belong to the kingdom, but it is not the simple addition of goods or possessions. "He makes it clear that the way of discipleship is not a reduction in what we already are, not an attenuation of our lives, not a subtraction from what we are used to," Eugene Peterson explained. "Rather he will expand our capacities and fill us up with life so that we overflow with joy."[8]

Jesus urged His followers to make the kingdom of God and His righteousness their priority (Matt. 6:33). Ultimate prosperity is more than a quality of life. Prosperity is life itself, and that life is found in Christ. The solution to greed is to retrain our desire. When we succumb to greed, it is not the nature of prosperity that becomes warped but the nature of our desire. A desire for more displaces our gratefulness for what God has provided and undermines our trust in the Provider. The focus of our devotion shifts from the Giver to what is given. This is why Colossians 3:5 calls greed idolatry.

This same verse says that the only way to deal with greed is by putting to death "whatever belongs to your earthly nature." The impulse of greed, like lust and gluttony, must be answered with denial. Since greed is never just a private sin, the path of refusal has both a private and a public dimension. It begins by saying no to our desires. This involves a turning away from the symbols of prosperity to the source. We must take Jesus at His word and accept that life does not consist in an abundance of things. We must be willing let go of the things we think we want and aspire to something better. We must learn how to be content. The Scriptures are clear that contentment this side of eternity is possible. They also make it clear that the only way to learn to be content is to recognize that you can be satisfied without getting everything you want. According to 1 Timothy 6:8, contentment requires having only the necessities: "But if we have food and clothing, we will be content with that." One reason we can do this is because we recognize the limits of our desires. We bring nothing into the world, and we can take nothing out of it (1 Tim. 6:7). The things we want cannot provide the ultimate happiness that we crave. Our own experience is proof of this. All the things we have wanted in the past have only opened the door to new wants. In the end, we will leave them all behind.

Turning away from greed is effective only when it is also coupled with a turning to God: "Keep your lives free from the love of money and be content with what you have, because God has said, 'Never will I leave you; never will I forsake you.' So we say with confidence, 'The Lord is my helper; I will not be afraid.

What can mere mortals do to me?'" (Heb. 13:5). Anxiety about the necessities of life is a trigger for greed. We are greedy because we are afraid. Those who know that God has promised never to forsake them have an answer for their fear. God will provide in the future just as He has provided in the past. His provision in the short-term is a reminder that He offers us something greater in the long-term. We look forward to an eternity in His presence.

The public dimension of our campaign of resistance against greed is the intentional practice of generosity. By giving we learn to let go. We learn to trust God's provision by becoming the channel through which He provides for others. We discover by experience the truth of Christ's words that it is "more blessed to give than to receive" (Acts 20:35). Those who give become more aware of the many ways that God provides for them. The pleasure of accumulating things is replaced by a different kind of thrill. We become participants with God in the great adventure of meeting the needs of others.

Paul's directions for the collection in the church of Corinth provide some practical guidelines for those who don't know how to begin practicing generosity. The regular practice of generosity begins with a plan. Decide how much and how often you want to give. For the Corinthians this involved the weekly setting aside of an amount that was in keeping with their income (1 Cor. 16:2). We might think of this as charitable budgeting. When you set aside a certain amount for your bills, set aside an amount for generous giving.

A second feature of your plan is to choose a recipient. To whom will you give? The Corinthians funneled their giving through the church. The church handed the funds over to Paul, who in turn delivered them to the needy church in Jerusalem. Some may want to give directly to individuals they know that are in need. Others may feel more comfortable channeling their giving through organizations that work with the poor.

A third important element in the Corinthian church's giving was that it was structured for accountability. Paul took steps to make sure that the donated funds were handled responsibly (1 Cor. 16:3–4). Churches and relief organizations should be open about how they use the funds entrusted to them. They should be willing to answer your questions and provide an audited financial statement that shows how they use their funds.

It doesn't matter what our net worth is. We are all prone to greed. How much is enough? The answer is always the same: just a little more. If greed is a form of idolatry then faith is its only true remedy. The fool in Jesus' parable thought that if he accumulated enough, his soul would be able to rest in those things (Luke 12:19). But rest is Christ's generous gift to all who trust in Him no matter how much we have (Matt. 11:28–30).

QUESTIONS FOR DISCUSSION:

1. How much is enough?

2. Why is it so easy to spot greed in others and so hard to recognize it in ourselves?

3. What concrete steps can we take to combat greed?

CHAPTER 5

Leisure:
Living Beyond the Weekend

My first job was short-term employment. I suppose you could say I was a day laborer. A neighbor hired me to weed her lawn. She provided me with a two-pronged weeding fork and promised to pay me five dollars when I finished. At the time, it sounded like a fortune. I said yes eagerly, carried away by visions of all the comic books I intended to purchase with the money I earned. Plus, this was work that I could do in a more or less recumbent position.

On my hands and knees in the hot sun, my enthusiasm soon diminished. The lawn looked much larger from that angle than I had first imagined. There were more weeds than I had thought. As the sweat trickled down the back of my neck, I poked them half-heartedly with the weeding fork, pausing every few minutes to scan the yard and see what kind of progress I was making. The view was not encouraging. The number of weeds appeared to be growing, not shrinking.

After a while, I persuaded myself that I had worked long enough. There was still a weed or two left, but surely my employer didn't expect me to pull every single weed. She did. "You're done already?" she asked in a skeptical tone when I went to the door to collect my money. Then she walked the lawn with me, pointing out the weeds that remained and grumbling about my work ethic. There were more than I thought. I wondered why I hadn't noticed them. Probably because they were the same color as the grass, I reasoned. With a sigh, I knelt down again and went back to work, this time with even less enthusiasm than before. Eventually, my employer paid me and sent me on my way, by now more eager to be rid of me than of the weeds. "A sluggard buries his hand in the dish; he is too lazy to bring it back to his mouth," Proverbs 26:15 observes. I suppose my unhappy employer would have said that a sluggard buries his hand in the lawn, too lazy to pluck out the weeds.

Os Guinness has said, "Sloth is so much the climate of the modern age that it is hard to recognize as a deadly sin." Guinness calls sloth "the underlying condition of a secular era."[1] In fact, in our leisure-oriented age, we kind of admire sloth. We smile at the person who has learned to game the system and can get others to do their work for them. It seems humorous, until we are being waited upon by a slothful person, or must depend upon that person for an important task. When we work with a slothful person and find that we must do their job as well as our own, it suddenly doesn't seem so cool.

These days, we have abandoned the archaic language of sloth. We call it leisure instead. Leisure is the ideal state for most of us. The ancients considered sloth to be a sin. We wonder what all the fuss is about. During the COVID-19 pandemic in 2020, many businesses were forced to shut down for weeks. Only essential employees were allowed to report for work. Despite the economic implications, not everyone was troubled by the change. One man I know laughed when I asked him about the emotional impact of not being able to go to work for so long. "It's like a dream come true," he said. He was only partly joking.

Our culture isn't worried about sloth. Labor unions lobby for a shorter work week. Commercials for money management firms entice potential customers with the promise of retiring early. We call it the good life. We believe the more time off we have, the better we will feel. We might be wrong. Psychologists warn that about 1/3 of the population suffers from something called leisure anxiety. According to some researchers, the line between having too much time on our hands and not enough is surprisingly thin. A study using data sets of over 35,000 people suggested that even though people feel they don't have enough time, too much time off causes people to feel anxious.[2] For people who work, the optimal amount was two hours a day. For those who didn't, it was four hours and forty-five minutes.

Neither the weekend nor retirement are necessarily bad. But we may be putting too much stock in both. Those who live for the weekend run the risk of squandering the blessings the other five days of the week. Some who expect retirement to be magical will discover that they have set their expectations too high. They will carry many of the concerns they had when they worked with them into retirement. Because they have never learned how to rest, their retirement may turn into a succession of empty hours. Or unexpected health or financial problems may suddenly intervene and rob them of the retirement dream altogether.

—

The sin of sloth has many features and manifests itself in many forms. At times it looks like what we call ennui, an immobilizing lethargy that leaches away our interest in those things that ought to concern us. When we are overcome by sloth, we may also squander our time and energy on meaningless trifles at the expense of other obligations. The stereotype of sloth is the person who won't get off the couch or doesn't want to get out of bed for work. But the problem is much larger. The way of sloth is a path full of ill-conceived shortcuts and ignored responsibilities. Sloth practices neglect under the guise of simplicity. It mistakes apathy for ease. Sloth is a sin of omission, but that does not necessarily mean that the slothful are inactive. Sloth is also a sin of rationalization. Those who ignore responsibility always have an excuse for not doing what they are supposed to do. A slothful person exerts the minimum required effort and would prefer to exert no effort at all. When they do make an effort, it is often under duress and is listless and half-hearted. Imagine the worst stereotype of the sort of service we receive at a bureaucratic hub like the division of motor vehicles, and you have a picture of sloth.

The sins of the slothful are a special focus of the book of Proverbs. Unlike the ant, which "has no commander, no overseer or ruler, yet it stores its provisions in summer and gathers its food at harvest," the slothful person refuses to take the initiative even when it is in their best interest to do so (Prov. 6:6–8). Sloth disposes a person to sacrifice the future on the altar of immediate gratification, even when doing so is ultimately disastrous (Prov. 6:9–11). The slothful person does not tend to even basic needs or responsibilities (Prov. 13:4; 19:24).

Sloth is selfish, but that does not mean that it acts in its own best interest. The sluggard is just as likely to ignore his own needs as anyone else's. The reasons given are often absurd: "The sluggard says, 'There's a lion outside! I'll be killed in the public square!'" (Prov. 22:13; see also 26:13). We tend to think of sloth as an addiction to rest but sloth is the antithesis of rest. The slothful person works hard at avoiding responsibilities, but that does not mean they can escape them. The sluggard who refuses to plow in season still needs food when harvest time comes (Prov. 20:4). The slothful person may ignore responsibilities, but that does not make those responsibilities magically disappear. The sluggard's problems become everyone else's problems. Others inevitably end up carrying the load. A life characterized by sloth is not a life of ease; it is a way "blocked with thorns" (Prov. 15:19).

Anxiety can also be a feature of sloth. Anxious sloth plays on our helplessness without pointing us in the direction of God's loving care or powerful support. Anxiety whispers in our ear each night but not in reassuring tones. Its counsels are counsels of despair. We think that the solution to our problems is more power or a change in our circumstances. But Jesus points us in a different direction. He urges us to view our powerlessness through the lens of faith. "Look at the birds of the air; they do not sow or reap or store away in barns, and yet your heavenly Father feeds them. Are you not much more valuable than they?" Jesus asks in Matthew 6:26–27. "Can any one of you by worrying add a single hour to your life?"

In 2 Thessalonians 3:11, the apostle Paul focuses on another form of sloth: "We hear that some among you are idle and disruptive. They are not busy; they are busybodies." Paul's criticism is proof that sloth can be active. Those he condemns were idle and disruptive at the same time. They were meddlers who did not tend to their own business but inserted themselves into affairs that did not concern them. If these are the same people Paul condemned in the previous chapter, they were theological meddlers who unsettled the church with false teaching about the return of Christ (2 Thess. 2:2). Although they claimed to speak for God, they did so without His authority.

Paul's criticism suggests that these self-appointed spiritual leaders expected to be supported by the church instead of working. They not only disrupted the church, but also took advantage of the church. It is not wrong for the church to support its ministers. In 1 Corinthians 9:3–12 Paul calls this a "right." Churches are obligated to provide for those who serve in the ministry of the Word (1 Cor. 9:14). This support is not charity. Both Jesus and Paul referred to it as a "wage" (Luke 10:7; 1 Tim. 5:18). Pastors are not mere employees but are workers. As such, they are subject to the same expectations God has of all workers, no matter what the calling. The obligation that Jesus and Paul speak of is a shared one. If the church owes the pastor a wage, the pastor owes the church a quality of work that is commensurate with that wage. The church is as worthy of the work as the worker is of the wage.

Elsewhere Paul expressed similar concerns about widows. Widows were an especially vulnerable class in an age when no forms of government assistance existed. During hard times, the family was the only available social safety net. Widows who met certain qualifications were eligible to receive financial support from the church (1 Tim. 5:3–8). By the second century, this practice had developed into an order of women who served the church but were not ordained. It eventually took on a more ascetic cast, but the practice was initially intended to care for widows who had no family to provide for them (v. 8). The qualifications Paul identified were both spiritual and practical. Before being considered, candidates must first prove that they were truly in need without others to provide for them. Their lives were to be marked by faith, prayer, and service. Paul directed that younger women be excluded lest they: "get into the habit of being idle and going about from house to house. And not only do they become idlers, but also busybodies who talk nonsense, saying things they ought not to" (1 Tim. 5:13).

Idleness is not a state of rest but one of self-indulgent neglect. Those who are idle are often busy but are not useful. Their contribution to any group effort is a distraction rather than a help. They do not attend to their own responsibilities but are eager to monitor and criticize the work of others. Those who succumb to idleness are prone to the sin of meddling. As is the case with most of the capital sins we have studied, the digital world of social media and the internet has increased our capacity for these sins. It has made it easy to squander time and energy that we could invest elsewhere more productively with a click or a swipe. The digital world can be useful, but it is not a neutral environment. At the dawn of the digital age, Neil Postman warned that every technology carries with it an ideological bias. Postman described this bias as "a predisposition to construct the world as one thing rather than another, to value one thing over another, to amplify one sense or skill or attitude more loudly than another."[3] The world of social media presents itself as a medium for social connection and communication. In reality, it is socially detached and given to simplistic thinking and sloganizing. The digital world gives us almost unlimited opportunity to be voyeurs and critics. We spend hours watching and reading intimate details about people we hardly know and affairs that have little to do with us. These are often matters that we would probably be better off not knowing, but we not only greedily consume the information but also share it with others. An earlier age would have called this gossip. Paul would have considered it meddling and considered us busybodies. We call it connecting and call ourselves friends.

The remedy for sloth is not merely to get busy. It is to discover what God has called us to be and do. We must understand the nature and value of work. The church needs a sound theology of work because sloth is often promoted as an antidote for work under the false rubric of leisure. The church also needs a theology of rest because our view of both work and rest has become diseased. As a result, we do not know how to do either. Our work has become a burden because we no longer consider it to be a way of serving God. The church's leaders are complicit in this because many pastors are as ignorant of what their congregation's calling is as the congregation is of theirs.

According to the *American Time Use Survey* published by the Bureau of Labor Statistics, Americans spend most of their time sleeping, working, and engaging in leisure activities (in that order).[4] The top leisure activity is watching television. Older people who are unemployed watch the most and parents with young children watch the least. Men watch more television than women, and everyone watches more on the weekend.[5] But in terms of experience, the lines between work and leisure are often blurred. The things we do for work look similar to the things we do on our time off. Many of the things we do during our time off, especially when it comes to domestic needs like cooking, cleaning, or caring for family, are a form of work. In American culture, busyness is a status symbol. The busier we are, the more successful we seem. Consumption is also a status symbol. These two are related for obvious reasons; if we earn more we can consume more. Work and consumption both invade the spaces we have set aside for leisure.

The same could be said of our sacred spaces. Today many churches employ the same strategies that businesses practice. They market themselves and carry out their ministries in competition with other churches. Most churches expect their members to do more than show up for worship. It is not enough to be Christian; they must also be Christian *workers* who add value to the church's enterprise.

On the other hand, many, if not most, of these Christians

feel like religious consumers. Church leaders usually blame the congregation for this, but it is not entirely the congregation's fault. Pastors chide church members for being religious consumers while at the same time treating them like customers. The overall effect is both confusing and demoralizing. The congregation is expected to represent the church's brand so that it can increase its market share and attract new attenders. Church attendance seems like an end in itself, and the charge of religious consumerism feels like a double standard. The church is concerned about the tastes of outsiders and newcomers, but the congregation is rebuked for having similar concerns. "Our vocations are bounded on one side by consumer appetites, on the other by a marketing mind-set," Eugene Peterson has observed. "Pastoral vocation is interpreted from the congregational side as the work of meeting people's religious needs on demand at the best possible price and from the clerical side as satisfying those same needs quickly and efficiently."[6] What Peterson describes is a kind of codependency between pastors and church members. Church members expect the church to provide spiritual goods and services. Church leaders rely on the church's members to market and staff the programs that deliver their spiritual product.

Meanwhile the spaces where we engage in work and leisure are often not addressed at all. Because their spiritual significance is unexplained, the congregation's regular employment and time off seem like spiritual dead zones. Neither has much value for the Christian life. The only work that matters is the work done on behalf of the church. Their leisure time has no spiritual value at all unless it is devoted to working for the church. Consequently, members feel pressured to sign up for a job in the church in addition to their regular jobs and use their time off to do ministry projects like short-term mission trips. Churches increasingly co-opt activities that were once assigned to the realm of leisure and uses them for ministry.

A church located near a baseball stadium adjusts its service time to accommodate fans who want to attend the game. Another makes viewing the football game part of its service during football season. Many host Super Bowl parties. Some churches have groups that work on crafts or play team sports that in a non-church context would be considered hobbies. None of these things is necessarily wrong. But they do seem to muddy the definition of ministry somewhat. If I watch the game in the church building, it is ministry. Is it still ministry if I simply invite my friends over to my house to see it? Does it have any spiritual significance if I watch the game alone? If a group who likes motorcycles departs from the church for a scenic drive in the country it is a "motorcycle ministry." If they leave from someone's garage and take the same route, it's only a ride.

———

When I was a pastor, I tended to think that the few minutes the congregation spent listening to me preach was most important hour of their week. How could it not be? I had labored on the sermon for many hours. I had prayed for them. I expected God to do something great. I also thought that, next to the sermon, their most important time was spent serving in the church's programs.

But as important as these may have been, most of their week was spent in other places doing other things. Where was God then? Eugene Peterson is right: "The sanctuary is essential, but it isn't the primary location for day-by-day cultivation and practice of spirituality, the Holy Spirit shaping the Christ-life in us."[7]

The landscape may be changing. Many seminaries have developed courses and seminars that address the connection between faith and work. The Kern Family Foundation has provided grants to schools to support activities that advance an integrated vision of faith, work, and economics. The Gospel Coalition's website has a section devoted to the subject.[8] But there is still much that needs to be done to help those in the church understand the connection between their ordinary work and their spiritual growth.

One reason for the disconnect may be due to a misunderstanding of the relationship between work and Adam's fall. After all, didn't God say, "By the sweat of your brow you will eat your food" (Gen. 3:19)? It is true that our work, like everything else in creation, has been affected by humanity's fall into sin. But work itself is not a punishment. According to the creation account, we were designed to work. Genesis 2:15 says that the Lord put Adam in the garden of Eden "to work it and take care of it." Eve was created to be Adam's partner in this divine calling (Gen. 2:20). Adam and Eve were more than gardeners; they were caretakers of the world God had created. From its very beginning, human work was intended to be an exercise of stewardship. Those who work are imitating their Creator who is also a worker. The wonders of creation are called the "works" of His hand (Ps. 8:6). God finished them in six days and "rested from all his work" on the seventh. Yet according to Jesus, He continues to work "to this very day" (John 5:17). If work were by its very nature a consequence of sin, it seems unlikely that we would find God engaging in such an activity.

Jesus, too, was no stranger to the world of work. Before beginning His public ministry the Savior submitted Himself to the daily grind. Jesus did not merely dabble in work. He became so proficient in the vocation of His earthly father, Joseph, that others knew Him by His trade before they knew of Him as a rabbi. The people of Jesus' hometown referred to Him as "the carpenter" (Mark 6:3). The dignity of work is seen in the fact that our Lord did not think it beneath Him to work for a living.

Income is a major motivation for working. Believers are commanded to work so that they will not have to steal and will have something to share with those who are in need (Acts 20:34–35; Eph. 4:28). Both motives share the same assumption. Those who labor do not work merely for the joy of the task. They expect to be paid (see 2 Tim. 2:6). While the notion of an earned wage is incompatible with the Bible's doctrine of salvation, it is the foundation for its doctrine of labor. Both Testaments teach that those who labor are owed an equitable wage. The Law of Moses stipulated that the hired servant's wages must be paid in a timely manner. Failure to do so was a sin (Lev. 19:13; Deut. 24:14–15). James later reaffirmed this in the New Testament (James 5:4). Even when the worker was an indentured servant, the money paid to them was viewed as their right. The New Testament reaffirmed this principle. Jesus was the first to introduce the metaphor of the "worker" into Christian ministry. According to

Christ the Christian worker deserves the wage (Luke 10:7). It is not a gift but is owed.

Not only is the worker worthy of the wage; what the employer pays must be in proportion to the service rendered. Indentured servants in the New Testament era were entitled to compensation that was "right and fair" for their work (Col. 4:1). This description outlines the two standards that govern the determination of any employee's compensation. First is the standard of righteousness. The employer's motive should not be to get the most for the least from those in its employ but to do "right" by them. Righteous compensation for work is not simply a question of economics. It reflects a commitment to the well-being of those who are employed. The command for a just return elevates the matter of employee salaries and benefits to the ethical realm. The other standard that shapes the employer's compensation to an employee is the principle of equity. Not only is compensation to be just, it must also be "fair." This implies a relationship between the nature and demands of the work and the return provided. Fairness is measured on two important levels. Is the compensation fair in view of the demands made upon the employee by the task? Is the compensation fair compared to what others are paid for similar work?

But this relationship is not one-sided. The worker also has obligations that correspond to that which the employer provides. An employee owes the employer "an honest day's work for a day's pay." An employer has a right to expect more than the satisfactory completion of assigned tasks from a Christian employee. Respect, appropriate compliance to the expectations and requirements made by those in authority, and diligence of execution are also part of what is due to those for whom we work. Sloth violates this mutual covenant of obligation and expects to receive what is owed without giving what is due.

Sloth is not only a sin of the workplace; it insinuates itself into every sphere of life where effort is required. Sloth can attach itself to the way we think, love, and play. It is that state of lethargy that always opts for the easy path. Sloth is the enemy of perseverance because it leaches away our capacity to persist in effort. Sloth is the handmaid of the hopeless. "In the world it calls itself tolerance; but in hell it is called despair," Dorothy Sayers observes of sloth. "It is the accomplice of the other sins and their worst punishment. It is the sin that believes in nothing, cares for nothing, seeks to know nothing, interferes with nothing, enjoys nothing, loves nothing, hates nothing, finds purpose in nothing, lives for nothing, and remains alive only because there is nothing it would die for."[9]

It would be a mistake, however, to conclude that the antidote for sloth is work. Work that has been detached from our larger calling in Christ can be as destructive as sloth. Derek Thompson suggests that, for many, work has become a kind of secular religion. They look to their work to find meaning in life. Thompson defines this secular religion, which he calls workism, this way: "It is the belief that work is not only necessary to economic production, but also the centerpiece of one's identity and life's purpose; and the belief that any policy to promote human welfare must *always* encourage more work."[10] Workism is a kind of idolatry. It is not God who is their highest good but work. Workism expects more from work than it can reasonably provide. If sloth diminishes the importance of work, workism does the opposite. Workism exaggerates the value of work beyond measure. In this view, we do not work to live, but we live to work. Those who place such high expectations on work set themselves up for disappointment. "The rise of the professional class and corporate bureaucracies in the early 20th century created the modern journey of a career, a narrative arc bending toward a set of precious initials: VP, SVP, CEO," Thompson explains. "The upshot is that for today's workists, anything short of finding one's vocational soul mate means a wasted life."[11] Those whose level of success falls short of expectations worry that they are doomed to lead unfulfilled and empty lives.

Christians have adopted their own version of workism by assigning ultimate meaning to a particular kind of work that is usually labeled ministry. The highest form is what is sometimes called vocational or full-time ministry. By this standard ministerial work is the noblest form of work. Martyn Lloyd-Jones is typical when he calls the work of preaching "the highest and the greatest and the most glorious calling to which anyone can ever be called."[12] He is not just speaking of the task of sharing the gospel but of preaching as a vocation. Lloyd-Jones, who had trained as a medical doctor, began his career as an assistant to the Royal Physician. He became a member of the Royal College of Physicians but soon became convinced that he had been called to preach. He left the medical profession and became a pastor.

There is no question that proclaiming the gospel is a great privilege. Preaching is one of the most important tasks in the life of the church. But if we say that full-time ministry is the highest vocation of all, what does this mean for the majority of Christians who are called to other vocations? How should factory workers, cooks, and cashiers think about their work? Obviously, not all work is the same. Some work is more difficult than others. Some work requires advanced training. Some work is morally questionable. Stealing involves work but is not a suitable vocation for a Christian. The biblical standard that makes work acceptable is that it contributes toward the good of the individual and the community at large (Eph. 4:28). There is immoral work, and even good work can be performed in an unethical manner. But any valid form of work has worth in God's sight.

Is there a difference between ordinary work and gospel work? Not in terms of value. Both have value in God's sight. Those God has not called to full-time ministry still bear witness to the truth of the gospel with their words and lives. If there is a difference, it is one of time, focus, and support. Those who are in full-time ministry have the privilege of devoting themselves to serving the gospel and the church without also bearing the responsibility of ordinary employment. Ministry is their ordinary work. In most cases, the focus of their effort is on the church. Their calling is to equip the church to bear witness to Christ in their individual contexts (Eph. 4:12). Because they serve the church, they are supported by the church (1 Cor. 9:14). Since their calling is to prepare God's people to fulfill their calling in the home, work-place, and neighborhood, it is essential for those in ministry to see the sacred value of common work.

The antidote for sloth is not effort but rest. Jesus offers rest as a gift to all who have worn themselves out in fruitless effort. "Come to me, all you who are weary and burdened, and I will give you rest," Jesus promises in Matthew 11:28. The rest of Christ also brings with it a vocation that Jesus describes by means of the surprising metaphor of the yoke (Matt. 11:29–30). What Jesus describes in these verses is not the vocation of professional ministry or even church work but something much larger. It is the vocation of discipleship. Those who receive the yoke of Christ accept His invitation to "learn from me." They place themselves under His tutelage, not only in the workplace or the church, but in every sphere of life. Although Christ's promise is one of rest, the metaphor He uses implies activity. The yoke was a farming implement, normally laid upon the neck of a beast of burden to enable them to carry the farmer's load. With this invitation, Jesus reverses the expected order when it comes to the relationship between work and rest. Instead of working our way into rest, Jesus promises a rest that energizes us in service to Him no matter what the activity.

Theologian Josef Pieper calls this "leisure." Leisure, in this sense, isn't merely time off, but a state of being that comes as a gift from Christ. "Leisure, it must be clearly understood, is a mental and spiritual attitude—it is not simply the result of external factors, it is not the inevitable result of spare time, a holiday, a weekend or a vacation," Pieper explains. He calls it an attitude of the mind and a condition of the soul.[13]

Another word for this rest is *grace*. By this definition, rest is as important to our work as it is to our play. Rest as God defines it is a state granted to all those who have ceased from their own efforts to be right with God (Heb. 4:10). Rest is not the end of all effort but the end of self-empowered attempts to earn God's favor. It is also the end of living for self alone. In the ancient world, the yoke was a symbol of slavery, and those who accept the yoke of Christ also accept their new status as His slaves (Eph. 6:6). Slavery to Christ is not indentured servitude. We are not working our way out of our obligation to Him. The Christian life is not a contractual arrangement by which we seek to earn God's grace and forgiveness after it has been given to us. The yoke places us, and all that concerns us, under the authority and control of the Savior. Our work, our play, our home life, and everything else is offered to Him as an act of worship (see Rom. 12:1–2). Jesus, in turn, exercises His gentle but absolute authority in those spheres, showing us what it means to live for Him in each of those spaces. We act as His stewards, representing His interests.

True rest is marked by an attitude of confidence and peace. It is grounded in trust and particularly in trust that rests in God. The essence of rest is expressed in Psalm 138:8: "The LORD will vindicate me; your love, LORD, endures forever—do not abandon the works of your hands." It is the confidence that comes from knowing, "that he who began a good work in you will carry it on to completion until the day of Christ Jesus" (Phil. 1:6).

QUESTIONS FOR DISCUSSION

1. What is the difference between rest and sloth? How can you distinguish between the two?

2. Why do you think our culture no longer sees sloth as a moral problem?

3. When do you find it most difficult to experience rest? Why do you think this is?

CHAPTER 6

Justice:
Life in an Age of Outrage

A saying attributed to St. Augustine goes, "Hope has two beautiful daughters. Their names are anger and courage; anger at the way things are, and courage to see that they do not remain the way they are." No one seems to know where or even whether Augustine actually expressed such a thought. To be honest, it sounds more like something a modern would say. The view of the ancients was much less approving of anger than in our day. The ancient attitude was more like the one expressed by the fourth-century desert father Abba Macarius: "If when you want to reprove someone you are stirred to anger, you are pandering to your own passion. Lose not yourself to save another."[1]

The old monk's restraint seems peculiar. Everybody gets angry. Some people deserve our anger. Anger is just an emotion, an expression of our righteous indignation. When it is rightly employed, anger can be the fuel that energizes change. At least, that's how we see it. Perhaps we are right in thinking this. As the words attributed to St. Augustine suggest, maybe anger really is the offspring of hope. Could anger be a fire kindled in the soul by a vision of a different world? Maybe the moderns have it right after all. We have removed anger from the list of deadly sins and declared it a virtue.

True justice is a biblical virtue and a foundational requirement of law. In the Old Testament, it was the primary responsibility of rulers and judges. The basic standard of justice is equity or impartiality. Justice applies the rule of law to all. The Scriptures warn of two main threats to this. One is individual, and the other is collective. Justice is undermined when some individuals are shown preference over others or are given a pass because of their position. This is sometimes the case of the wealthy and privileged. The Law of Moses warned judges not to ignore the concerns of the poor (Ex. 23:6). But the same law also warned judges not to show favoritism to a poor person in a lawsuit (Ex. 23:3). Justice can be subverted by the mob. Exodus 23:2 warns those who judge not to "pervert justice by siding with the crowd." We understand the warning about ignoring the poor. The other two dangers emphasized in these verses seem odd to us, especially in an age where talk about justice so often relies upon the judgment of the crowd, and attempts to "level the playing field" involve showing preference to those who have historically been slighted. Leviticus 19:15 echoes the warning of Exodus 23:1–3: "Do not pervert justice; do not show partiality to the poor or favoritism to the great, but judge your neighbor fairly." The Hebrew phrase that is translated "partiality" in this verse is one that means to "lift up the face." Perhaps the image pictures the poor person face down in supplication. To lift someone's face was to show them favor. The other Hebrew phrase used to speak of partiality to the rich differs slightly. The phrase translated "favoritism" is one that literally means "to honor the face." One speaks of action and the other of disposition, but both are a form of sinful favoritism. The former is a kind of reverse discrimination based on social or economic hardship, while the latter is a matter of privilege that grows out of wealth or status. The Mosaic law considered either to be a perversion of justice.

The collective threat to justice comes from the crowd. Justice can be subverted by pressure from the multitude. Exodus 23:2 warns those who judge not to "pervert justice by siding with the crowd." Since the standard of biblical justice is righteousness, a measure that is established by God, the boundaries of what constitutes just behavior are not subject to the whims of the majority. In Scripture, righteousness is a matter for conformity, not consent. Today's justice warriors have a very different view. We live in a vigilante culture where those who don't like the outcome of due process take matters into their own hands. This view essentially equates justice with bullying. This is true whether it is a virtual mob, whose posts on social media endeavor to shout and shame, or a literal mob that surrounds someone whose views they oppose to intimidate. In its harmless form this anger is often little more than sentimentalized outrage. At its most damaging it is the rage of the mob. Indeed, many use the phrase "twitter mob" to describe these kinds of attacks. One study by researchers from the University of Wisconsin found that 15,000 bullying tweets are posted per day on Twitter.[2] Ironically, it may not take a multitude to make a cybermob. According to a recent study by the Pew Research Center, only 10 percent of users are responsible for 80 percent of what is posted on Twitter.[3] But when this narrow band of voices is targeted at a single person, it can have the force of a bullet.

Anger has been rehabilitated in today's outrage culture, so that many now consider it to be healthy. Ryan Martin, chair of the psychology department at the University of Wisconsin at Green Bay, is an example of this changed perspective. "Just as your fear alerts you to danger, your anger alerts you to injustice," Martin observed in a TED Talk entitled "Why We Get Mad—And Why It's Healthy." "It's one of the ways your brain communicates to you that you have had enough. What's more, it energizes you to confront that injustice."[4]

Is there an upside to anger? On the surface, the warning of James 1:20 seems absolute. Everyone should be slow to become angry because "human anger does not produce the righteousness that God desires." But if this is true, then what are we to make of the anger of some of the saints of old? Or of Jesus? Moses was angry when the Israelites ignored his directions about the collection of manna and tried to save some of it for the next day (Ex. 16:20). He was "very angry" when Dathan and Abiram questioned his authority to lead the people (Num. 16:15). Nehemiah was furious when he learned that the poor exiles who had returned to Jerusalem to rebuild the wall were exploited by the rulers, nobles, and wealthy returnees. Some were so poor that they were forced into indentured servitude to make ends meet (Neh. 5:6). When the Jews in Corinth became abusive to the apostle Paul, "he shook out his clothes in protest and said to them, 'Your blood be on your own heads! I am innocent of it. From now on I will go to the Gentiles'" (Acts 18:6; see also Matt. 10:14). If this did not signify some measure of anger, it at least indicated strong feeling!

But we don't need to look any further than Jesus to find that there is such a thing as virtuous anger. According to Mark 3, the religious leaders watched to see whether Jesus would heal a man with a withered hand in the hopes that they could accuse Him of violating the Sabbath. The rabbis taught that the sick could be treated on the Sabbath, but only when their life was in danger. Aware of the Pharisees' intent, Jesus told the man to stand before the congregation. Jesus asked them, "Which is lawful on the Sabbath: to do good or to do evil, to save life or to kill?" When they refused to answer, Jesus "looked around at them in anger" (Mark 3:5). Mark 10:14 describes Jesus' indignation when the disciples rebuked those who brought little children to Jesus so that He would lay hands on them and pronounce a blessing.

Jesus' anger is an extension of the ultimate expression of virtuous anger: the wrath of God. The notion of a wrathful God has largely fallen out of favor. This is true even among those who believe that such wrath exists. We treat God's wrath the way we would the awkward personality trait of some family member. We hardly ever talk about it. We would rather not think about it. Instead, we attempt to put the best face on a bad situation. Sure, He flies off the handle once in a while, but that's not really who He is. He is a good guy once you get to know Him. Yet we cannot grasp the Bible's view of justice without taking the wrath of God into account. God's wrath is not a divine personality flaw but a measure of the distance that sin has introduced into our relationship with Him.

Both testaments speak of God's anger. Psalm 7:11 says, "God is a righteous judge, a God who displays his wrath every day." Hebrews 10:31 warns, "It is a dreadful thing to fall into the hands of the living God." Much of the book of Revelation depicts the outpouring of God's wrath on the earth (Rev. 14:10; 16:19). Understanding what this means for God's character is more difficult than simply noting the language the Bible uses to describe it. Some analogy between God's anger and ours is clearly intended. The Bible speaks of a shared experience. Yet when we compare God's anger with ours, there are some fundamental differences. Human anger is an emotional reaction to some stimulus. It springs from circumstances that are beyond our control. When our goals are frustrated, or we feel that we have treated unfairly, our anger is triggered. While we can learn to control the way that we respond to our anger, we cannot control the fact that we experience it. We cannot say the same of God. He is never powerless. As the psalmist puts it, "Our God is in heaven; he does whatever pleases him" (Ps. 115:3). The fact that we are sinners justifies God's wrath. It also interjects the fatal flaw into our anger. The greatest difference between human anger and God's anger is that we possess a sinful nature, and God does not. Human anger is not always sin, but it is always affected by our sin. Our fallen nature skews our perspective in our favor. This bias makes us highly sensitive to the offenses while leaving us blind to our own (Matt. 7:3–4).

How, then, should we view God's anger in light of our own? Jesus Christ is proof that emotions are not incompatible with a divine nature. The Bible's talk about divine anger is not anthropomorphism. We should not think of the God of the Bible as if He were like the pagan gods of antiquity. The gods of Greek and Roman mythology behaved like humans with superpowers. Their lust, pettiness, jealousy, and spitefulness matched the worst of human excesses. Neither should we treat the wrath of God as if it were mere hyperbole. God's anger is not like that of a human parent who threatens without intending to punish. God's wrath is not a dumb show of force intended to frighten us into submission. His anger is real.

Theologians find it easier to accept the fact that the Bible speaks of God's emotional character than to explain its nature. In our attempts to explain it, we face three temptations. The first temptation is to dismiss the idea altogether. Some have argued that God has no emotional dimension at all to His nature. However, theologian J. I. Packer explains that the theological doctrine of divine impassibility does not have anything to do with God's emotional detachment but with God's relationship to suffering. To say that God is impassible means that God's capacity to enter into the suffering of His creatures is voluntary. As Packer so vividly puts it, "he is never his creatures' hapless victim."[5]

The second temptation overshoots the mark by assuming that God's emotions and ours are identical. We get angry, but God gets really, really angry. The trouble with this view is not its suggestion that God's anger exceeds ours but in its anthropomorphism. It assumes that the only difference between God's anger and ours is a matter of scale. The result is a view of God that makes Him seem like a bully or an abusive parent. Yet those who attempt to follow the middle path between these two extremes may find that they stumble over the third great temptation. It is a view of God's wrath that is so nebulous that it is essentially meaningless. Such a God hardly seems worthy of the level of fear Jesus spoke about. "I tell you, my friends, do not be afraid of those who kill the body and after that can do no more," Jesus warns in Luke 12:4–5. "But I will show you whom you should fear: Fear him who, after your body has been killed, has authority to throw you into hell. Yes, I tell you, fear him."

That God does have some dimension of His character which corresponds to what we call emotion is the inevitable conclusion for anyone who takes divine self-revelation seriously. The Bible often uses emotional language when it speaks of God. It does so in such human terms that we are sometimes disturbed by the thought. This is especially true of those emotions we consider to be negative, like anger. Our problem is not that we can't relate to such references but the opposite. We are all too familiar with these kinds of feelings and believe that God should rise above them. We can accept that God might feel a measure of irritation at times, as any superior being might with an inferior. But the notion of wrath seems too uncontrolled, especially when it is attended by flames, plagues, stinging serpents, and cataclysm. We may tell ourselves that those who suffer such things probably deserve them, but deep inside we harbor a lurking uncertainty about the whole thing. It all just feels a little too out of control.

The key to unlocking this dilemma is not found in a philosophical formula but a person. Although Jesus possesses two distinct natures, one that is truly divine and one that is truly human, these two distinct natures are joined in one person. The human does not diminish the divine, and the divine does not negate the reality of the human. Yet these are not two separate Christs but one person.

One result of this union of two natures in a single person is that it helps us understand God in human terms. Hebrews 1:3 says that Jesus is "the radiance of God's glory and the exact representation of his being." He is "the image of the invisible God" (Col. 1:15). Jesus enables us to glimpse what God is like by putting a human face on the divine nature.

The Bible's statements about God's wrath must be viewed through the lens of the divine attribute of immutability. The psalmist speaks of immutability when he compares God to the variableness of all that God has created: "They will perish, but you remain; they will all wear out like a garment. Like clothing you will change them and they will be discarded. But you remain the same, and your years will never end" (Ps. 102:26–27). God does not have a variable emotional disposition like ours. He does not get "bummed out" or fly into a rage and then later decide that He has acted rashly. He "does not change like shifting shadows" (James 1:17).

It may also aid our understanding of God's anger to move in the same direction that C. S. Lewis does when he attempts to imagine the nature of heaven. In *The Great Divorce*, Lewis describes a heaven where all the analogous delights of earth are infinitely heightened. The features of Lewis's heavenly landscape are like those of earth but also substantially different. The flowers and grass are diamond-hard. The realities of heaven as Lewis imagines them are so substantial that all that is of the earth is mere shadow and ghostly imitation by comparison. Likewise, Lewis imagines a hell that is so diminished by the heavenly that it is smaller than one pebble of the earthly world and smaller even than one atom of the "real" heavenly world. Might not a similar dynamic be true when it comes to the affective nature of God?

Instead of viewing God's emotions simply as mirrors of our own, we ought to see our emotions as signposts that point toward something in God, which is infinitely higher, purer, and more solid. In this view, the line that connects our emotional nature with God's moves from the lesser to the greater. We are like God, but He is not like us. Where God's anger is concerned, this is a comparison with a narrow focus. The Bible's language of divine wrath is intended to remind us of what it is like to be in an oppositional relationship with God. We know what it is like to be the focus of someone's displeasure and to experience rejection. The emphasis is not on God's emotional state so much as it is on our position. Sin makes us God's enemies. He is opposed to us because we are opposed to Him. Unrighteousness always places us at cross purposes with God so that we cannot be in harmony with Him (2 Cor. 6:15).

Perhaps most important, it is a mistake to consider God's wrath apart from all the other aspects of His character. When we isolate God's wrath from His attributes of righteousness, love, and mercy, we distort His image. God is just and would have continued to be just if He had decided to leave humanity to suffer the consequences of sin. Yet God is also merciful. These two attributes do not work against each other in God's character. They operate in harmony. In the believer's experience, each of these serves the other. God's justice reveals our need for grace and mercy. God's grace and mercy, displayed through the saving work of Christ, enables us to be made just. Romans 3:25 calls Jesus a propitiation, a term was used to speak of a sacrifice that atones for sin and satisfies divine wrath. Jesus' suffering was a display of God's justice and the means by which sinners were made righteous. In this way, God was able to "be just and the one who justifies those who have faith in Jesus" (Rom. 3:26). What is more, God's method for dealing with sin was not to dismiss His righteous standard but to absorb the penalty Himself by pouring it out on His Son.

—

The rhetoric of justice has become commonplace in our day, both inside and outside the church. But a common definition of what we mean by the term is hard to find. For some people, justice means racial reconciliation. For others it speaks of economic restructuring and redistribution of wealth. Those who serve meals in the homeless shelter, others who work with victims of human trafficking, and people who disrupt traffic on the expressway to protest police shootings all believe they are working for justice. Most of the time, justice is only a philosophical abstraction until it is made concrete for us in personal experience. Usually, the way this happens is through a personal experience of injustice.

According to C. S. Lewis, we have these experiences all the time, especially when we are arguing with someone. Lewis notes that people often say things like, "'How'd you like it if anyone did the same to you?'—'That's my seat, I was there first'—'Leave him alone, he isn't doing you any harm'—'Why should you shove in first?'—'Give me a bit of your orange, I gave you a bit of mine'—'Come on, you promised.'"[6] When we respond this way, we are appealing to an innate sense of justice. It is a sense that underneath everything, there is some commonly understood rule of fair play. When that rule is violated, even in a trivial way, we feel instinctively that there ought to be consequences. When there aren't consequences, our natural response is to get angry. Usually we don't call it anger. We prefer the label "righteous indignation." But if we are truly honest with ourselves, we are forced to admit that there is often more indignation than righteousness in our anger.

Prince Felix of Schwarzenberg, foreign minister of Austria, was discussing what should be done with the captured rebels after the Hungarian revolt was suppressed in 1849. When someone suggested that it would be wise to show mercy toward the rebels, Schwarzenberg agreed. "Yes, indeed, a good idea," he said, "but first, we will have a little hanging." Too often this is the spirit in which we carry out our quest for justice.

We are like Jonah, God's furious prophet, hunkered down on the outskirts of Nineveh, watching to see what God will do. This is waiting, but it is not patience. We are weary of God's patience. We are tired of waiting. Mercy is fine, but first we would like to see a little justice. What we don't recognize is that our notion of justice may not agree with God's. As Christians, we have grown comfortable with the language of grace. It is a part of our vocabulary. The nomenclature of grace is embedded in our hymnody. We sing, "Only a sinner saved by grace" or "Amazing grace, how sweet the sound, that saved a wretch like me." We say these things about ourselves, and we feel good about it. We enjoy the experience of God's grace. But while we sing about grace, what we desire is many cases is retaliation. Like the man in Jesus' parable, we rush out from the king's presence, with the words of absolution still ringing in our ears, and find our fellow servant who owes us. We grab them by the neck and begin to throttle them crying, "Pay back what you owe me" (Matt. 18:28). This is the spirit of justice. It's not that we despise the notion of mercy. How could we? By all means, let us show mercy. But first, we will have a little hanging.

The desire of justice is legitimate, as are many of the concerns of those who call for it. Unfortunately, what we call justice can also be nothing more than sentimentality expressed in the form of anger. This sentimentalized quest for justice trades on impatience. It misrepresents evil, not by denying its existence, but by oversimplifying its nature. We ignore difficult complexities in favor of a superficial diagnosis, which becomes a stereotype. The emotional self-indulgence of our anger is evident in our rhetoric, which usually gives off more heat than light. We are quick to speak, slow to listen, and too intellectually impatient to do the hard work of analysis that is needed to understand the nature of the problem or divine a solution. We are willing to shout, carry a sign, or post to social media. But that's about as far as our plan of action goes. Anger is our only real contribution to the cause.

It is not wrong to desire justice, not even for ourselves. The longing for justice is a frequent theme in the Psalms. Like the psalmist, we want to know why it is taking so long for God to set things right (Ps. 13:1–3; 94:1–3). Disappointment mixed with delay is a breeding ground for anger. The problem with our impatience is that we soon find that we cannot force God's hand. We cannot bend His will to ours. We cannot accelerate His timetable. Like it or not, we are compelled to wait. What is more, we are not the only ones who must do this.

The Scriptures tell us that heaven itself is waiting for justice. When the apostle John opens a window on the worship of heaven in Revelation 6:9–10, he gives us a glimpse of the souls who were slain for the Word of God. Their struggle is over. They are at rest, and yet even in this blessed state they still cry out to God for justice. God's answer, John tells us, is "wait a little longer" (Rev. 6:10–11). Justice, it turns out, is the unfulfilled ambition of heaven.

What does this mean for our quest for justice? We might be tempted to wonder whether it even makes sense to work for justice. The answer of the church to this question down through the ages is also the answer of Scripture itself. It is a resounding, "Yes!" Micah 6:8 shows us what this looks like in practice: "He has shown you, O mortal, what is good. And what does the Lord require of you? To act justly and to love mercy and to walk humbly with your God." Those who act justly also love mercy. The antidote for the cheap justice of our modern age is the threefold remedy prescribed in Micah 6:8. It is action that is shaped by mercy and carried out in humility.

To act justly is to do the right thing. For the Jew, this meant conformity to the standards of God's law. For Israel's rulers, it involved the application of the law's provisions and demands across all sectors of society. But the obligation to act justly was not exclusive to those who governed. Micah's examples of unjust behavior include many drawn from daily life. They weren't limited to the sins of rulers or even the rich. They are sins of the marketplace and the family as well as the ruling powers (Micah 6:10–11; 7:5–8). Justice is the burden of the state, but it is also the obligation of the individual. Justice is a concern from the boardroom to the bedroom.

Many of today's justice warriors tend to focus primarily on broad social structures like institutions and organizations. Systemic problems are real. But systems are not sentient. They are created by and changed through the actions of individuals and groups. This is why the Bible calls for just behavior on a personal as well as collective level. When we focus only on abstract social constructs like institutions and organizations, we shift the burden to a realm that is too nebulous for concrete action. Justice becomes the responsibility a vague "someone" rather than specific individuals. It is certainly not my responsibility. In such a climate, my only obligation as an advocate for justice is to express my outrage. Governments, institutions, and organizations can indeed be unjust, but it is individuals who enact that injustice, and only individuals can correct it. Individuals can hide behind systems and organizations to commit or profit from injustice, but they can also change them. William Wilberforce, the sixteenth-century politician, whose efforts contributed greatly to the abolition of slavery in the British Empire, is proof of the power of the individual to change systemic injustice.

There is an even more catastrophic obstacle facing us in our quest for justice. It is the fact that we are, by nature, fundamentally unjust. The New Testament language of righteousness speaks of a particular kind of righteousness: the righteousness that comes to us from God through the person and work of Jesus Christ. God, who has established righteousness as His standard, is also the only source of the righteousness He requires. By sending Jesus Christ to be a sacrifice of atonement, God was able to maintain His standard of righteousness while providing righteousness to those who had none of their own. God is the only one who has a right to feel righteous indignation. He keeps the accounts and He alone can execute ultimate justice. The day of vengeance belongs to the Lord (Isa. 34:8; 61:2). But God is also the only one who can satisfy His wrath. He is the Just One and the one who justifies because the only righteousness God will accept is His own. To "do justice" in this New Testament sense means much more than social activism. It means that we will reflect Christ's righteousness in our ordinary lives by the power of Christ. Doing justice is not a matter of living up to God's standard but one of living out that standard through the empowerment of the Holy Spirit.

To act justly in this Christian sense also means to act out of mercy. This includes specific acts of mercy, but it also involves more. The command of Micah 6:8 is to "love" mercy. The Lord calls for more than a practice of almsgiving. To love mercy is to cultivate a merciful disposition. The Hebrew word that the NIV translates "mercy" in Micah 6:8 is one that is associated with God's character (see Ex. 20:6; 34:7; Deut. 5:10). The word could also be translated "kindness" or "loving-kindness."

Mercy's chief characteristic is patience. Mercy waits and does not move quickly to enact a deserved penalty. In Jesus' parable of the unforgiving servant, the plea of both debtors is the same: "Be patient with me" (Matt. 18:26, 29). When the unforgiving servant demanded payment from his fellow servant, the master called him in. "You wicked servant," he said. "I canceled all that debt of yours because you begged me to. Shouldn't you have had mercy on your fellow servant just as I had on you?" (18:32). Jesus told the parable to illustrate His answer to Peter's question about the limits of forgiveness: "Lord, how many times shall I forgive my brother or sister who sins against me? Up to seven times?" Jesus answered Peter, "I tell you, not seven times, but seventy-seven times" (18:21–22).

Peter's question exposes the fatal flaw in our hunger for justice. It it not only skewed toward self-interest, but also chiefly concerned with payback. Like Peter, we want to know where to draw the line. The justice that Micah 6:8 describes is one tempered with mercy. These two seem to be incompatible. After all, isn't justice all about making sure those who have done wrong get what's coming to them? "Sin and retribution belong together," Helmut Thielicke observes. "This is logical."[7] The biblical call to show mercy to others, both in Micah 6:8 and in Jesus' parable, is grounded in the fact that we have received mercy from God.

A well-loved hymn says, "Oh to grace how great a debtor daily I'm constrained to be."[8] This is the secret to showing mercy. Not forgetting the offense but recalling our own debt to grace. Those who belong to Jesus Christ do not show mercy to others because they deserve it. They do not. We do not show mercy because someone has finally come to understand what they did wrong and how much it hurt us. They often have no clue. We do not even show them mercy because others want it from us. Sometimes they do not. We show mercy for our own sake. We forgive because God has forgiven us.

As a purely theoretical idea, mercy sounds great. We can all get behind it. But things are different when the person who calls for your mercy is that boss who took credit for your good idea or that sister-in-law who made such unreasonable demands when your mother passed away. It is easy to be in full agreement with what Jesus says as long as His words remain abstract and theoretical. But approving of mercy and actually showing mercy are two very different matters.

As a result, instead of showing mercy, we sometimes resort to creative accounting. We offer counterfeit mercy instead of the real thing by minimizing the debt owed to us. "Oh, it was nothing" we say. "It doesn't matter. I'm bigger than that." The trouble with this approach is that our inner accountant is still keeping track. Interest on the debt is compounded, and I know exactly how much owed to me. Or we may try to stretch out the payments. We give those who have offended us a pass for the day. Yet as we walk away, we think to ourselves, "I don't get mad, I get even. You won't get yours today, but it will be payday someday!" We might renegotiate the debt, but we are unwilling to cancel it altogether because the offense that was committed against us was real. It was not merely perception. If we cancel the debt, who will look out for our interests? The answer, of course, is that God does.

Mercy is not comfortable. If we are going to show mercy, we must relinquish our claim on the debt that is owed us and trust God to make up the difference. We must also have a clear sense of how much we have been forgiven. Mercy may bring a sense of loss, but it is also a gateway to freedom. When we show mercy, we often discover that we are as bound by the debt as the offender. Mercy enables us to understand the grace that God has shown to us. We are not attempting to pay God back when we refuse to call in another's debt. Mercy is a testimony of grace received.

C. S. Lewis is right. We all have an innate thirst for justice. What is more, we know the price for violating the law of fair play. That, too, is imprinted on our soul. It is the fundamental law of all debt. It is eye for eye and tooth for tooth. You pay what you owe. Pay every penny of it, and all the interest, too! But it is just here that our passion for justice starts to break down for us. I can call in your debt against me, but I also have debts of my own. This is the fundamental dilemma of justice. If I call in your debt, I convict myself. If I show mercy, I relinquish my claim and risk suffering loss. Doing justice with mercy requires grace, and grace implies loss. I cannot exercise this kind of justice without leaving the debt in God's hands.

The mercy-infused justice that Micah calls for, and that Jesus illustrates, includes a third crucial feature. It demands an awareness of God. Micah 6:8 says that to do this you must "walk humbly with your God." The stereotype of a humble person is that of someone who has a low view of themselves. The biblical notion speaks of a different kind of self-awareness. It is the sort that Paul counsels in Romans 12:3: "For by the grace given me I say to every one of you: Do not think of yourself more highly than you ought, but rather think of yourself with sober judgment, in accordance with the faith God has distributed to each of you." What does the apostle mean by "sober" judgment? Sober judgment is a realism that has been informed by God's grace. To think of myself with sober judgment is to see myself through God's eyes. It takes my weaknesses and failures into account, but it also takes note of God's provision.

However, the most important awareness that Micah 6:8 mentions is an awareness of God. It is worth noting Micah's use of the possessive: "walk humbly with *your* God." The sober judgment of Christian humility includes a recognition of our position in Christ. Jesus has reconciled us to God, removing all grounds for enmity, and making us His children. We do not walk with God in cringing fear like slaves who have been let off the hook but just barely. Rather, "as dearly loved children," we "walk in the way of love, just as Christ loved us and gave himself up for us as a fragrant offering and sacrifice to God" (Eph. 5:2).

———

Not long after I started driving, I had to go to court over an automobile accident. It wasn't a big one, just a fender bender. But it was my fault. I hit a patch of ice and slid into an oncoming vehicle. There were no injuries, and the damage to both cars was repairable. Still, the driver of the other car was angry. As the police officer wrote me a ticket and told me that I needed to appear in court, the other driver assured me that he would be there to make certain that I received the highest penalty.

I was terrified as the date approached. I'd never been to court before and wondered what the punishment might be. Looking back on it now, I suspect it would have been minimal. The judge certainly wouldn't have given me jail time for a dent. But to me, it felt like a major offense. The worst part of it was that I knew I was the one at fault. I had misjudged the curve. I was driving too fast for the conditions. What verdict could the judge render on my behalf other than guilty? I felt ashamed.

When my father asked me how I was going to plead, I told him that I planned to admit my guilt. "I am a Christian," I said. "I can't lie about it." He was furious. "You stand there, and you tell the judge you are innocent," he demanded. When I told him I couldn't do such a thing in good conscience, he swore and walked away, muttering something about my faith.

When my court date arrived, I took my place on an uncomfortable wooden bench and waited to be called. I felt torn between the demands of my conscience and the desire to please my father. As I listened to the other cases, I noticed that most of them were like mine, minor accidents that were a result of bad weather. I also noticed that many of the defendants didn't admit to either guilt or innocence. When asked for a plea, they stood silent. "Do you stand mute?" the judge asked? When they answered yes, the judge told them that a plea of not guilty would be entered on their behalf.

At last, my turn came. I stood before the judge's raised bench and shook as he reviewed the details of my case. "How do you plead?" he asked. "I stand mute," I replied. The judge looked around the courtroom. "Is the driver of the other vehicle present?" he asked. Nobody answered. "Is the officer who wrote the ticket in the courtroom?" the judge inquired. He was not. "Case dismissed," the judge curtly declared.

The wave of relief that swept over me was palpable. It felt like mercy, but it was not. The judge dismissed my case on a technicality. He could not declare me guilty because there was nobody there to testify against me.

Mercy is something else. Mercy belongs only to the guilty. For the Christian, mercy is not a verdict. It is a person. Because Jesus took our place, God's verdict of righteous for the believer is no mere legal fiction. When the Bible calls us righteous, it means what it says. For this reason, the word that the Bible uses to describe God's verdict is not mercy but justice. By sending Jesus to stand in my place, God was able to be both "just" and "the one who justifies those who have faith in Jesus" (Rom. 3:26).

It is only through this lens that we can understand what it means to be just in the biblical sense of the word. Justice is not outrage. Neither is it revenge. Justice is righteousness, which is first received as a gift and then displayed as a testimony to God's grace. It is the habit of walking with an awareness of God's goodness, knowing that He has shown us mercy and empowered us to do the right thing. Justice is an act of faith that trusts God to look out for our interests. Justice is the offspring of hope that has two beautiful daughters. Their names are grace and truth: "For the law was given through Moses; grace and truth came through Jesus Christ" (John 1:17).

QUESTIONS FOR DISCUSSION:

1. What is justice?

2. Why do you think people are so concerned about justice today?

3. How does true justice differ from "sentimentalized outrage"?

4. What is the relationship between justice and grace?

CHAPTER 7

Envy:
Getting What's Coming to Them

When I was growing up, my parents used to buy my shoes at a little shop at the end of our block. There was something about the store's big chairs with their smell of leather that made the place seem luxurious to me. This was before the days of big box stores and discount shoe chains. Getting a new pair of shoes was always a big deal, an event that warranted a family expedition. It was also a minor drama whenever the new shoes were for my brother or sister instead of me.

"But honey, you don't need a new pair of shoes," my mother explained, in a vain effort to stem the flood of tears I unleashed. Her reasoned argument brought me no comfort. Not as long as the shiny gleam of a sibling's new shoes was in plain sight. My anguish was not about need. It was about possession. As long as they had what I did not, I was certain that I could not be happy. I might never be happy again.

Envy is the devil's little hammer, bending our hearts until it turns us against anyone who possesses what we want. Envy poisons our desires and weaponizes them. Envy is part of a constellation of sins that the apostle Paul labels the acts of the sinful nature or "the flesh" (Gal. 5:19–20). This makes it kin to hatred, discord, jealousy, selfish ambition, dissensions, and factions. New Testament scholar F. F. Bruce has defined envy as "the grudging spirit that cannot bear to contemplate someone else's prosperity."[1]

These days envy is a brand used to sell any number products, ranging from perfume to health care to computer printers. The same "materialistic porn" on reality TV that appeals to our greed is also designed to provoke envy. While it may still be considered bad form to admit to envy in polite society, contemporary culture has legitimized envy in many ways. Why *do* we post so often about ourselves on social media? We do sometimes share about our failures and struggles. But we are far more likely to post about our cute kids, remarkable spouse, new home, or great vacation. It is certainly no sin to celebrate God's blessings in our lives. Maybe we are only trying help others learn how to "rejoice with those who rejoice" (Rom. 12:15). Yet might there not also be a darker motive in play? Could it be that we not only want people to rejoice with us, but also secretly hope that they will wish they *were* us?

In a culture where everyone who competes gets a trophy, envy isn't just legitimized, but sometimes institutionalized. Of course, envy is not called envy in these cases. It goes by other names. We may call it sensitivity or fairness or leveling the playing field. "Resentment and hatred at the individual level are obvious and unsurprising, though still quite sobering," Os Guinness observes. "But envy is less often traced at the public level where it has enormous consequences in many areas—for example, the excessive egalitarianism of all socialism and some forms of modern democracy, the excesses of affirmative action, the barely concealed appeal of progressive taxation and much advertising, the twisted motivation of therapeutic victim playing, the rage for rights and entitlement, the destructive tearing down by gossip columns and television 'gawk shows,' and the fact that Western societies are becoming increasingly angry, fueling a disturbing culture of rage, while Western elites commonly display signs of guilt said to serve as ways to avoid envy."[2]

Envy collaborates with pride and anger. It was envy in part that prompted Jesus' disciples to argue about which of them should be considered the greatest (Mark 9:34). Pride motivated the Corinthians to divide into factions over their favorite teachers but these distinctions were also intended to make those who identified with others jealous (1 Cor. 1:12). Envy can even be a motive that drives our ministry (Phil. 1:15). Have you ever noticed how hard it can be to rejoice when someone else's church experiences more success than your own? James 3:14 reveals that we can become so comfortable with the presence of envy that we boast about it!

But as is true of the other dangerous virtues we have studied, the ancients had a very different view. "Envy, you should know, is a disease more difficult to cure than any other sin," the fifth-century monastic leader John Cassian warned. "I would almost say that once a man is poisoned by it there is no antidote."[3]

The ancients considered envy to be Satan's sin. It caused him to covet God's throne and His glory (Isa. 14:13). Envy was also the implicit motive embedded in the first temptation. Satan imputed envy to God as the explanation for the prohibition of the forbidden fruit: "For God knows that when you eat from it your eyes will be opened, and you will be like God, knowing good and evil" (Gen. 3:5). Satan implied that God had kept for Himself something that should also have belonged to Adam and Eve.

Envy was the motive for the first murder recorded in the Bible. When the Lord looked with favor on Abel and his offering, Cain grew angry enough to kill (Gen. 4:4–6). The Hebrew text says that God "gazed" at Abel's offering, indicating that Cain was angry because God ignored his offering. Cain expected that his offering would secure God's favor. He thought it was owed to him. This expectation was not born of faith but arrogance. When the Lord questioned him about what had happened to Abel, Cain answered as if God were merely a servant (Gen. 4:9). His offering was a sham (1 John 3:12).

Like Cain, envy is a bitterness that springs from false assumptions about what is owed to us. It claims the favor that God has bestowed on others for ourselves. Envy is the anger we feel when we believe we have been overlooked. Someone else gets the benefit that should have been ours, and we are left standing on the sidelines.

Envy drove Joseph's brothers to sell him into slavery (Gen. 37:3–4). Envy was the motive that caused Aaron and Miriam to challenge Moses' authority (Num. 12:2). When Saul grew envious of David's praise, his admiration turned to fury (1 Sam. 18:1–11). It made Ahab an accomplice in Naboth's murder (1 Kings 21:1–16). Envy drove the Jewish religious leaders to hand Jesus over to the Romans (Matt. 27:18).

Envy is a kind of greed, but it is a particular mode of greed. Greed wants. Envy wants, too. But envy wants what belongs to someone else. Envy desires what it wants *because* it belongs to someone else. As is apparent from these biblical examples, anger is a common byproduct of envy (Ps. 37:1, 7, 8). Envy is the indignation we feel toward those who have what we think should have been ours. But ultimately it is an outrage that is directed at God Himself. This sense of outrage is fueled by a conviction that the prosperity, opportunity, or blessing that we desire has gone to the wrong person. God seems to have squandered His goodness on those who are not worthy of it. Envy leads to comparision, which is always skewed in our favor. We convince ourselves that those who have what we desire haven't worked as hard as we have. They are not as qualified as us. They do not deserve what they have, or they do not appreciate it. If it is left unchecked, this outrage can turn to hatred and despair.

———

Envy is the sin of the "have-nots." But that does not make it primarily a sin of the poor. The sin of envy is so ingrained in our fallen nature that it renders everyone a have-not. In the book of Ecclesiastes, Solomon says that envy drives most human achievements (Eccl. 4:4). Sometimes what we call ambition is only envy dressed up in business clothing. We know that envy is bad, but we admire ambition. Not all ambition is evil, of course. In its benign form, ambition can help us to clarify a target of legitimate desire and energize us to do what is necessary to satisfy it. It is even possible to have spiritual ambitions. Paul was eager to preach the gospel where it was not known (Rom. 15:20). He made it his life's goal to please God (2 Cor. 5:9). The apostle made plans and took the initiative. Sometimes his plans were interrupted by God, who redirected the apostle and set him on a different route (Acts 16:6–10).

But sin tends to distort our ambitions until they grow cancerous. When legitimate ambition grows out of control, our sense of entitlement grows with it. Even spiritual ambitions can be twisted by jealousy or self-interest into a form of envy. Some who preached Christ in Paul's day did so out of "selfish ambition" (Phil. 1:17). The Greek word that is translated "selfish ambition" in this verse had its roots in the custom of hiring people to work as day laborers. It is a word that describes the motives of those who act selfishly out of their own interests. These teachers did not serve the interests of the kingdom but built a personal following. They saw Paul as a rival and hoped that he would note their success and be troubled by it. They not only preached out of envy, but also hoped to provoke Paul to envy with their success. Paul includes selfish ambition in the list of the deeds of the flesh (Gal. 5:20–21).

Consequently, envy is a gateway sin, opening the door to a host of other sins in the community of believers, like jealousy, anger, dissension, and evil. The Bible often speaks of envy in conjunction with jealousy. The two are related, but there is a subtle difference between them. Jealousy can sometimes be legitimate. For example, jealousy is an attribute of God (Exod. 20:5; 34:14; Deut. 4:24; 5:9; 6:15; Josh. 24:19). The Scriptures characterize God's jealousy as a kind of holy protectiveness. God's jealousy is the rationale for the commandment that forbids idolatry. Since He alone is God, He alone is to be worshiped. The biblical language of divine jealousy also implies a protective sense of possession where His people are concerned. The Lord's exclusive claim to humanity's worship does not spring from ego, insecurity, or some divine need to be appreciated but by His benevolence. God needs nothing from us, not even our devotion (Ps. 50:9–15; Acts 17:24–25). We are the ones who benefit from worship.

Virtuous jealousy is a legitimate feeling of rightful interest, ownership, or possession. A spouse who feels jealousy when their partner has been unfaithful is justified. But human jealousy, like ambition, can be distorted by sin. Paul was "jealous with a godly jealousy" for the Corinthians, but he also included jealousy in the list of the deeds of the sinful nature (2 Cor. 11:2; Gal. 5:20). The context determines whether jealousy is legitimate. Sinful jealousy is an expression of envy. The one who succumbs to it feels possessive for something over which they have no proper claim.

Sinful jealousy will fracture the church. In Corinth, believers divided into groups that identified with specific teachers. First Corinthians 3:3–4, depicts what today we might call a celebrity culture. Corinthian believers drew spiritual distinctions between themselves based on their affiliation with "big name" preachers and teachers. Those who made a claim "I follow Paul" or "I follow

Apollos" weren't saying that they shared the high moral character as their heroes. These were merely labels they used to distinguish themselves from those who identified with anyone else. The implication of these labels seems clear: "Since my teacher is better than your teacher, I am better than you!" They were intended to provoke others to jealousy and make others feel inferior.

Paul corrected their flawed thinking by suggesting alternative labels. Instead of viewing themselves as "spiritual," they needed to recognize that such behavior only proved that they were immature, "mere infants in Christ" (1 Cor. 3:1). Provoking one another to jealousy was not the mark of spiritually advanced people. Such behavior was a mark of those whose values and actions had been shaped by their sinful nature. They were "worldly," or as the Greek text says, "fleshly." They considered themselves to be spiritually superior. Instead, Paul told them that they were behaving like "mere human beings" (1 Cor. 3:4).

The apostle also urged the Corinthians to think differently about their teachers. Instead of viewing their teachers as spiritual celebrities and superheroes, they should see them for what they were: "Only servants, through whom you came to believe—as the Lord has assigned to each his task" (1 Cor. 3:5). There are no spiritual superstars. Only slaves and servants who complete the tasks assigned to them by Christ.

Today's church is just as divided as the Corinthians were. We also identify with our favorite preachers and teachers. In some cases, they are Christian celebrities whose teaching we follow and promote. In others, it may be the unknown pastor of our little church, which we are certain is better than all the other churches in town! Our differences are also cultural and political, but the message is the same. It is better to be us than to be them. When we elevate these secondary identities in a way that dismisses or marginalizes other believers, we are not acting as people who live by the Spirit but as people who are still worldly—mere infants in Christ. When we identify those with whom we differ by using demeaning labels or make snarky comments about them on social media, we are not demonstrating our spiritual superiority. We are not even relevant. We are fleshly.

In today's tribalized society, we often lean into secondary identities more than our core identity in Christ. These may be ethnic, regional, or national. They may revolve around our favorite political party, theological orientation, or style of worship. It is understandable that we would have differences over such matters. The problem comes not necessarily when we disagree with others but treat them with contempt. Maybe it reflects only a poor choice of friends on my part, but many of the Facebook posts I read seem to intentionally tweak the nose of those with whom they disagree. They call their opponents by unflattering nicknames. The current political climate has not helped matters, where opponents on both sides ridicule and demean one another. It is unfortunate that this same spirit has crept into the church.

It is not wrong to have high regard for those who minister God's word to us (Heb. 13:7). Nor is it wrong to express our Christian identity through the many secondary identities that God has gifted to us. We can demonstrate our devotion to Christ in many distinctive ways through our gender, ethnicities, or nationalities. We can also be Christian artists, athletes, and professionals. We may even express our devotion through some of the differences that shape our denominational, ecclesial, and theological traditions. But no matter what label we claim for ourselves, our most important identity is that of being in Christ.

The example of the Corinthian church is a solemn reminder that jealousy and envy find an ally in our ego. Envy is quick to judge and eager to find fault. Envy has as much to do with the way we see ourselves in relation to others as it does with the things we desire. Envy isn't just interested in possession. It is also interested in one-upmanship. As a result, we are most vulnerable to envy when we compare ourselves to our peers. Most of us don't envy Bill Gates's billions. We envy those who are like us. We envy the colleague who got the promotion that might have been ours or the neighbor whose child attends a more prestigious school than ours does. The pressure of envy comes from a desire to surpass. But envy wants to do more. Envy prefers to surpass others in a way that shows them that we have eclipsed them.

—

Although our envy often causes collateral damage to those we envy, its worst effect is on the heart of its host. "As rust wears away iron, so envy corrodes the soul it inhabits," the fourth-century theologian Basil of Caesarea noted.[4] Basil's warning echoes Proverbs 14:30: "A heart at peace gives life to the body, but envy rots the bones." For those who are afflicted with it, envy is a pain we will feel every time our neighbor prospers. "If his neighbor's land is fertile, if his house abounds with all the goods of this life, if he, its master, enjoys continual gladness of heart—all these things aggravate the sickness and add to the pain of the envious man."[5]

There is more to envy than merely desiring what someone else has. If my neighbor buys a new car and I decide to purchase the same model, I am not necessarily acting out of envy. If I admire my neighbor's home or their job, I may not be succumbing to envy. Envy is about displacement. The Bible commands, "Rejoice with those who rejoice; mourn with those who mourn" (Rom. 12:15). Envy so twists our desire so that we do the opposite. We mourn when others rejoice and rejoice when they suffer misfortune. Envy infuses desire with spite. Spite unites itself with our ordinary desires in a way that blinds us to envy's deadly nature and distorts our view of those who have what we want. "Tormented not by the faults of the people they envy, but by their prosperity, they cannot admit the truth about others and are always on the watch for trivial and silly causes of offense," John Cassian explains. "These imaginary causes of offense cannot be overcome so long as the deadly virus is in them and they will not bring it to the surface."[6] Envy is a kind of anxiety. It is an agitation of desire that combines lust with fear. Psalm 37 links envy and fretting (Ps. 37:1, 7, 8). The Hebrew word for "fret" speaks of a quaking fear. Those who succumb to this sin are afraid that they will be deprived of what should be theirs.

Envy is destructive to the soul, even when the perceived inequity is real. The fact that the people I envy do not deserve what they have does not make my envy less destructive. Asaph was envious of "the prosperity of the wicked" (Ps. 73:3). Even though they did not deserve their prosperity, Asaph saw his envy of them as a sin. Asaph's struggle with envy caused him to wonder whether his efforts to maintain a pure heart and righteous practice had been in vain (v. 13). Envy sours the heart, leaving us embittered toward those we envy and ultimately toward God (v. 21). It makes us insensible of God's goodness. "When my heart was grieved and my spirit embittered, I was senseless and ignorant; I was a brute beast before you," Asaph lamented (vv. 21–22). As long as we remain in this blinded state, there can be no recovery.

We cannot simply talk ourselves out of envy. We must be delivered from it by God. Some try to argue themselves out of envy by remembering that others are worse off than they are. This sort of reasoning says, "I cried because I had no shoes until I met a man who had no feet." But this is just a reconfigured form of envy that makes us the winners after all. "I may not have what I want," it says, "but at least I have more than that guy!" Asaph points us in a different direction. He recovered from envy by attaining a clearer vision of God (Ps. 73:17). When Asaph entered the sanctuary, he understood the fate of the wicked whose prosperity he coveted. He also saw the true nature of his envy.

Recovery from envy begins with illumination. God must open our eyes so we see our desire for what it truly is. Envy is a kind of ambition, to be sure, but it is "selfish ambition" (James 3:14). The focus of sinful ambition isn't limited to material things. It often occurs in the spiritual realm. The kind of ambition James warns about disguises itself as wisdom. Those who are driven by this ambition use God's truth to advance their own interests. They claim to be preaching the kingdom of God, but their real aim is to build a kinglet of their own. Selfish ambition infects spiritual zeal with the toxin of comparison and competition. Selfish ambition is not defined by congregational size. It is equally at home in the house church as it is in the megachurch.

Selfish ambition is the sin of Diotrephes, "who loves to be first" (3 John 9). It can be found in ordinary Christians as often as in church leaders. It is the spirit that drives both gatekeepers and gate-crashers. It can find its way into the church's kitchen as easily as it does the church's board meetings. Selfish ambition is a sin of measuring. Those who have been poisoned by it "measure themselves by themselves and compare themselves with themselves" (2 Cor. 10:12). Because they are their own standard, they always come out on top. But the game is rigged. The reason they compare themselves to others is so that they *will* come out on top. The outcome was settled before the comparison even began. Selfish ambition produces a climate of cannibalistic spirituality where believers "bite and devour each other" (Gal. 5:15).

If we are to recover from the sin of envy, God must also change the way we think about those we envy. This may be the most difficult aspect of envy because envy skews our perception of others, persuading us that we deserve what they have more than they do. But we do not see others as they truly are. We do not even know ourselves for what we are. Such thinking usurps God's role as judge. More importantly, envy's skewed perspective fails to take into account God's goodness. He "causes his sun to rise on the evil and the good, and sends rain on the righteous and the unrighteous" (Matt. 5:45).

The antidote for envy combines faith, hope, and love. Faith

is the essential element because envy's power lies in its ability to cause us to question God's goodness and the wisdom of His provision. Envy exaggerates our desire until we become convinced that we cannot live without the thing we desire. Envy collaborates with lust and anger to build a false case against the one we envy and ultimately against God Himself. Envy tries to convince us that we are fatherless orphans who must fend for themselves. Faith brings us back to our senses and gently invites us to question these assumptions. We know what we want, but we do not always know what we need. Faith is the voice of Christ, which reminds us that we have a heavenly Father who knows what we need. Faith is Christ's gentle rebuke pointing out that, while there are many things we want, there is only One that is truly necessary. It urges us to choose the good portion and leave the rest in the Father's hands.

Hope bases its expectation on this confidence in God. It is not the crass hope of the prosperity gospel, which barters with God and trades devotion for trinkets. Instead, hope that is shaped by a biblical faith welcomes God's promises "from a distance" (Heb. 11:13). It is the settled assurance that God will do all that He has said. It is a conviction that true happiness does not lie in the things we desire but in God Himself.

When we fix our hope on God, we find the freedom to love those we envy. This does not mean that we automatically feel better about them. Biblical love is not fairy dust that we sprinkle over our emotions to make all the bad feelings we have about people disappear. The dislike that envy instills in us toward others may continue, at least for a time. Biblical love does not begin with a good feeling but with a disciplined decision to speak about and act toward others according to the rule of Christ. Love, in this sense, isn't necessarily a strong sense of affection, although that may come in time, but a disposition to act.

How, then, do we act toward those we envy? At first, we can only act in accordance with our feeling toward them. Our envy has made them enemies to us, so we must treat them as if they *were* our enemies. Jesus has shown us how we should deal with our enemies by giving two simple commands. The first is to pray for them (Matt. 5:44). The second is to greet them (Matt. 5:47). These two very basic actions link our inner world to the outer. When we pray for those we envy, we counter envy's natural desire to dispossess others with a dynamic of grace. When we pray for them, we seek the good of those we envy. We are praying for their blessing. By doing so, we also lay bare the cold reality of our envy before the presence of God. We cannot help it.

When we greet those we envy, we introduce the same counterforce of grace into our daily interaction with them. Few things are more basic to social interaction than a greeting. To refuse someone a greeting is a kind of dismissal. It is a denial of their existence. In Jesus' day the most common form of greeting was also a pronouncement of blessing: "Peace be with you" (Luke 24:36; John 20:19, 21, 26). According to Jesus, the act of greeting is more than a social form, it is a bold act of gracious inclusion. "If you love those who love you, what reward will you get? Are not even the tax collectors doing that?" Jesus warns in Matthew 5:46–47. "And if you greet only your own people, what are you doing more than others? Do not even pagans do that?"

In other words, Jesus is doing more than telling us to wish good morning to those we consider to be our enemies. There is more to this than a moment in the service when we shake hands and "pass the peace" to one another. He calls us to treat those we would normally regard as enemies and outsiders as if they were "our own people." How do we carry this out in practice? We do not make a distinction between them. We do not treat our friends one way and those we envy another. We do not exclude them from our interest or our conversation. We wish them well without sarcasm. We congratulate them for their accomplishments.

Recovery from envy requires that we redirect our focus and reprioritize our desires. Eastern religions like Buddhism and Hinduism look for the extinction of desire. This is a hopeless quest. God created us to desire. "We are primordially and essentially agents of love, which takes the structure of desire or longing," James K. A. Smith observes. "We are essentially and ultimately desiring animals, which is simply to say that we are essentially and ultimately lovers."[7] The key to defeating envy is not to suppress our capacity for desire but to reorient it. Jesus doesn't teach us to eradicate our desires but to subordinate them to the kingdom (Matt. 6:33). We overcome envy by submitting ourselves to God's order for our lives. Envy is an implied accusation against God, which suggests that He has been asleep at the wheel and has allowed things that should have been ours to go to others. Seeking the kingdom first is not a matter of adding Jesus to all the other things that are important to us and then trying to find time for Him. Instead it is a matter of recognizing that our heavenly Father will provide us with all we need and that what we need most is the ultimate reorientation of our desires. Jesus characterizes this reorientation as righteousness.

We don't need to stop desiring. Our desires need a conversion. This is true of desire in general, but it is especially true of envy. Envy is a kind of idolatry that values the gift more than the giver. Envy reaches out for what God has not given because it "regards the paltry pennies and miserable crumbs more highly than the hand that bestows them."[8] Asaph's turning point in his struggle with envy came when he entered the sanctuary and shifted his focus to God. There he was able to lift his gaze from those things he desired but did not have to the God who supplied his need: "Whom have I in heaven but you? And earth has nothing I desire besides you" (Ps. 73:25).

The answer to envy is happiness, and ultimate happiness (what the philosophers used to call felicity) is obtained as a gift, not by effort. "Happiness is essentially a gift; we are not the forgers of our own felicity," theologian Josef Pieper observes.[9] The lie of envy is that we can make ourselves happy by what we achieve or possess. The path to happiness does not begin with a vision of what we can achieve but with a sense of what God has given to us. Envy cannot be tamed; it can only be thrown down. The longing for what others have, along with its corresponding desire to dispossess them of those things, can be eliminated only by suffering a kind of death. We must accept the loss in order to discover the gain. This is the message of the beatitudes (Matt. 5:1–12). It is key to understanding Christ's warning in Mark 8:36: "What good is it for someone to gain the whole world, yet forfeit their soul?" This is how ambition works in the strange economy of the kingdom. Only the losers win.

QUESTIONS FOR DISCUSSION:

1. Is it always wrong to want what someone else has? Why or why not?

2. How can you distinguish between healthy desire and the sin of envy?

3. How does envy affect our relationships? What is the best way to deal with envy?

CHAPTER 8

Pride:
Why God Needs to Put Us in Our Place

W̲e live in an age that considers confidence to be a virtue. Some of us have been told since childhood that we are unique, above average, and destined for greatness. I understand what is going on here. Those who do this hope to strengthen their child's self-confidence. But I can't help wonder whether we are promising too much when we say such things. I suspect that the ancients would have used a different word to describe this kind of thinking. They might have called it hubris or pride. Instead of viewing it as the secret to success, they regarded hubris to be the fountainhead of all other sins. We feel differently. We don't want a low view of ourselves. We don't think it's healthy. Spend too much time talking poorly about ourselves, and we worry that in a few years, we will find ourselves in therapy working on our inadequacy issues. But I suspect that a little self-contempt might be healthy. If not contempt, then at least we might leave room for just a smidgen of self-doubt.

In some cases, pride is an emblem. Say the word *pride*, and many immediately think of the LGBTQ movement. Some link the term with their nationality or ethnic identity. Others use it to celebrate their favorite sports team. *Pride* is a noun, but it also functions as a verb. Pride isn't just about how we feel; it's something we do. We are proud. More than this, in today's culture, pride is no longer a reason to feel awkward. We no longer shuffle our feet and mumble about our accomplishments. We buy an ad. We post on social media. We aspire to pride. Most Christians believe there is a respectable version of pride. In today's culture, pride can be considered a virtue as much as it is seen as a personality flaw. Jessica Tracy, a professor of psychology at the University of British Columbia who specializes in human emotions, calls pride a "virtuous" sin. She has called pride "one of the most important motivational forces propelling human achievement."[1]

Tracy acknowledges that pride can sometimes take destructive forms like narcissism. She argues that narcissistic pride isn't really about pride at all, but it's the opposite. "In short, the narcissists' extreme arrogance is a cover-up," she explains. "The pride that narcissists experience—a pride that's best summed up with words like *arrogance, conceit,* and in Italy, *orgoglio*—is not about feeling good; it's about *avoiding feeling bad.*"[2] The arrogant pride of the narcissist is a cover for insecurity. Tracy distinguishes this darker or hubristic pride from its more constructive counterpart, which she labels authentic pride. The difference between them is a matter of accomplishment. "Authentic pride is the emotional response to successes that are hard won and that people know occurred as a result of their own efforts," Tracy explains. "Hubristic pride is the emotional response to successes that are perceived as less effortful and thus less controllable, events that, people believe, occurred simply because of who they are."[3] In general, however, Tracy considers pride, at least its authentic form, to be a quality worth cultivating. "My advice, based on the accumulated research evidence, is this: Seek out authentic pride," she urges. "Find a way to feel good about your best *me* self."[4]

Earlier generations of Christians would have been puzzled by such thinking. They did not consider pride to be a virtue but regarded it as chief among all the capital sins. "In what, therefore, can I justly glorify myself, and why should I look to be thought great?" the thirteenth-century Christian mystic Thomas à Kempis asked. "Truly, vainglory is a perilous sickness, a grievous pestilence, and a very great vanity, for it draws a man away from the true joy he should have in God and robs him of all heavenly grace."[5] In the third century, monastic leader John Cassian warned, "To do anything with the aim of increasing our reputation is to lay up treasure on earth; to hide it, and bury it where demons will eat it, vanity will corrode it like rust, pride will ruin it like moths: and the man who hid it will gain nothing from it."[6]

These leaders were merely echoing a theme they recognized from Scripture. The Bible condemns vain pride. Yet it does not condemn all forms of pride. For example, Scripture seems to acknowledge certain natural forms of pride. Proverbs 17:6 recognizes family pride when it asserts, "Children's children are a crown to the aged, and parents are the pride of their children." The Hebrew text literally says that fathers are the "glory" of their children.

Glory, in this sense, is something or someone that is a reason for boasting. Pride is a kind of magnification that draws attention to its object. It can be focused on someone else, like the child who glories in a parent. Or it can be self-focused. In general, glorying in self is frowned upon. "Let someone else praise you, and not your own mouth; an outsider, and not your own lips," Proverbs 27:2. Pride in the accomplishments of others is encouraged but not self-promotion. Yet the warning in this verse comes with a surprising corollary implication. While it is unwise to praise yourself, one may accept the praise of another.

In the New Testament, Paul shares the Old Testament's generally negative assessment of pride. He uses several terms to speak of sinful pride, but the action that epitomizes it most for Paul is that of boasting. It is not the act of boasting, but its object that is the problem. Paul was eager to boast or "glory" in the Corinthians (1 Cor. 15:31; 2 Cor. 7:4). He expected to do so "in the day of the Lord Jesus" and believed that the Corinthians would reciprocate (2 Cor. 1:14). But the apostle did not expect this to be a mutual celebration of personal achievement. Paul's boasting, whether it was about his own accomplishments or those of others, was ultimately a form of glorying in Christ (Rom. 15:17).

Unlike the "authentic" pride that Jessica Tracy advocates, which feels good about our best self, Paul's pride deflected the credit. Paul did not deny what he had accomplished, but he did not take credit for it either. The credit ultimately belonged to Christ. This gospel-based pride feels good about what God has done in and through us because we are in Christ. Because the credit belongs to Christ, this mode of pride rejoices just as easily in what God has done through others. The fact that the credit for his achievements belonged to Christ enabled Paul to experience a very different kind of self-pride: "If I must boast, I will boast of the things that show my weakness" (2 Cor. 11:30). This kind of anti-pride glories in those conditions that highlight God's power (2 Cor. 12:9).

Surely it is possible to have a legitimate sense of accomplishment without falling into sinful pride. The artisan can take pleasure in what their hands have created, and the athlete in the knowledge that they have done their best. If the worker is worthy of his keep, as Jesus says in Matthew 10:10, then by implication the work itself also has value. There is nothing sinful about feeling good about a job well done.

On the other hand, the partisan spirit of the Corinthian church shows that focusing on one's accomplishments, even those of others, can be dangerous. The apostle warned the divided church not to be "puffed up in being a follower of one of us over against the other" (1 Cor. 4:6). This corrective helps us grasp better the nature of sinful pride. It is more than a positive feeling about oneself; sinful pride is the assertion of self over another. It is an elevation of ourselves that draws an unwarranted distinction with others and assumes a position of superiority. Pride celebrates false achievements. Where there has been a genuine accomplishment, sinful pride takes too much credit (1 Cor. 4:7). Pride inserts the self where it does not properly belong.

—

Pride was Satan's premier sin (1 Tim. 3:6). Consequently, it was the sin that drew Adam and all creation with him into bondage to sin. Pride is the fountainhead of all the deadly sins. All the other sins flow into this one, and pride is the head-water from which all sin issues. This is a more expansive and subtle view of pride. We tend to think of pride only as conceit. Those of us who still consider pride to be a sin, or at least a serious personality flaw, have a tendency to think of it in a cartoonish way. Pride is the besetting sin of buffoons and blowhards. We think of the proud person as someone who has a big head. But there are many more socially acceptable and subtle forms of pride. Pride can be attractive as well as repulsive. We often mistake pride for confidence. The last decade has seen the public failure of several prominent church leaders whose brash confidence was part of their initial appeal but who later proved to be narcissists and bullies.

No church that is looking for a pastor says to itself, "Hey, I know! Let's hire a conceited jerk!" Churches give a lot of thought to the characteristics they want to see in their pastor, and most of them are good. Nobody who decides to attend a church is thinking, "Where can I find an abusive pastor today?" The church is drawn to narcissistic leaders because they appeal to us. Narcissistic leaders have a presence. They are exciting. They hold out the promise of great things for the church. Many produce impressive results, at least for a while. Those who see through the hype recognize it as pretentiousness. But for churches who are hoping for a messianic leader, narcissistic style can be very appealing. These churches are willing to tolerate the abuse in the hope that the pastor will lead them into the promised land of ministry success.

Any codependent relationship is built upon a dysfunctional system of rewards. We enable narcissistic behavior because we get something from the leader. Sometimes the reward is small. It may only be that we are addicted to the adrenaline of crisis that comes with this style of leadership. Or maybe we like the pastor's preaching. Churches tolerate narcissistic leadership behavior because they fear that no one else will be able to produce the same results. Churches with narcissistic leaders are often so identified with the pastor that his departure will have a negative effect on attendance. The larger the church, the more difficult it is to disengage because there seems to be so much at stake.

Churches enable narcissistic leaders by developing social systems that reinforce their abuse. Narcissistic leaders surround themselves with other leaders who make them feel special. This inner circle experiences a vicarious thrill by being associated with the leader. Because narcissistic leadership comes with perks and special treatment, the inner circle often gets rewarded along with the leader. The result is a codependent loop that blinds those who should be responsible for holding the narcissist accountable.

Narcissistic leaders are bullies. They develop organizational cultures that are marked by fear and punishment. Church members who question their agenda or practices are accused of being divisive and undermining God's plan. In a misapplication of 1 Samuel 26:9–11, those who criticize the pastor are sometimes warned not to "lay a hand on the Lord's anointed." Threats and retaliation are explained away as "church discipline." Narcissists use the power of their spiritual position to shut down anybody who challenges them. They create a culture of fear that silences objections and penalizes objectors. There is always a cost to those who challenge a narcissistic leader.

We should not, however, think of pride as a sin primarily of leaders. If we consider pride to be the sin of only big personalities in large places, we show that we do not understand pride at all. We also prove that we do not understand ourselves. Pride is the grain that runs through every sin. It is the thread that links all sin together. There is more to pride than promoting ourselves at the expense of others. Pride is ultimately an attempt to supplant God. This was the terrible twist in Satan's promise to Adam and Eve in the garden of Eden. The bait he offered to incite our first parents to sin was the hope of being "like God" (Gen. 3:5).

The cruel irony in this false promise was that Adam and Eve already possessed this gift in some measure. They had been created in God's image (Gen. 1:26–27). Their desire to be like God was not sinful, but the means proposed by Satan to achieve this end was. By refusing to heed God's warning and obey His prohibition not to take of the forbidden fruit, they claimed the right to rule themselves. Sinful pride compels us to act as if we are gods unto ourselves. Pride is the assertion of self over God. It involves the expansion of ourselves in our effort to marginalize God. Since pride is the grain that runs through every sin, it is also the grain that runs through every sinner. Everybody has a problem with pride.

We like to think of pride as the peacock of the capital sins, easily recognizable by its gaudiness and preening. But pride takes many forms. It is just as comfortable in rags as it is in garments of splendor. Speaking in the voice of the master tempter Screwtape,

C. S. Lewis points out, "All virtues are less formidable to us once the man is aware that he has them, but this is especially true of humility."[7] This observation exposes the essence of pride. It is not pride's self-exaltation but its self-consciousness that makes this sin so deadly. Pride is more than a person whose gaze is turned in on himself. Pride is a person who has become absorbed with himself.

Like so many of the sins we have looked at thus far, today's culture of social media seems especially suited for pride. After all, what could be more self-absorbed than expecting people to read your thoughts as you think about yourself? Well, perhaps video blogging, which expects people to watch you as you talk out loud about yourself. There are some people who engage in this sort of listening and get paid for it. We call them psychiatrists, psychologists, and pastors. Most wives do the same thing but for free. The self-absorbed, on the other hand, don't listen to anybody, unless they are listening to hear themselves praised.

This narcissism may be the most debilitating side effect of pride. The perspective of the narcissist is the point of view expressed by Haman in the story of Esther, who thought to himself, "Who is there that the king would rather honor than me?" (Est. 6:6). Haman is the villain of Esther's story, but in many ways, he is also the person with whom we can most easily identify. We might dislike Haman if we encountered him on the street or in the workplace. Yet there is something so familiar about the astonishment and shame Haman felt when he learned that the king intended to honor someone else that one is tempted to feel a pang of sympathy. Who has not felt the same shock and dismay at being overlooked? He "rushed home, with his head covered in grief" (Est. 6:12). The narcissist cannot bear to go unnoticed. While we may not be narcissists in the clinical sense of the word, there is a predisposition to narcissism in everyone who has been touched by Adam's sin.

Those who are self-absorbed are genuinely mystified when others accuse them of being self-centered. They do not consider themselves to be narcissists. They view themselves as benefactors and martyrs. They believe they have earned their position at the center of all things through personal merit, hard service, or simply by their existence. It does not occur to them that they would be anywhere else.

Pride's bent toward self-focus and entitlement shows how deeply envy and pride are intertwined. It is hard to see where one ends and the other begins. Does envy lead to pride, or do the assumptions of pride create an environment where envy takes root? The answer is yes. Haman was grieved over Mordecai's elevation because he saw Mordecai as an enemy who had bested him. Haman was enraged when Mordecai refused to kneel and pay homage to him (Est. 3:5). This is another feature of the narcissism that pride instills. It is a self-absorption that tolerates no rivals. Haman was afraid of Mordecai. He worried that Mordecai's rise in fortune foreshadowed a reversal in his own (Est. 6:12–13).

Pride, however, does not always produce narcissistic personalities in the classic sense. Sometimes it moves in the opposite direction. Pride can be understated as often as it is brazen. This adaptability is one of the things that makes pride so pervasive.

What passes for humility can be just as self-absorbed as stereotypical narcissism. The poster child for humble narcissism is Uriah Heep in David Copperfield. "A person like myself had better not aspire," Heep declares. "If he is to get on in life, he must get on umbly, Master Copperfield!"[8] Heep is a caricature we might easily recognize in others but whom we would find it difficult to identify in ourselves. The portrait of pride we find in him is an extreme one. Too extreme to serve as a mirror for our own. Our ventures into the realm of humble pride tend to be more subdued than Uriah Heep's over-the-top exclamations, but they amount to the same thing. Narcissistic humility is a peacock adorned with shabby feathers, but it is still a peacock. Pride is inveterately competitive. Even the drab narcissism of Uriah Heep will vie with others for the lowest seat at the table.

This also helps us to see how humility differs so radically from pride and how our thinking about humility can be distorted because of our pride. Humility is not thinking poorly of yourself. It is thinking away from yourself. Humility does not teach us to hate ourselves but it does teach us how to get over ourselves. Humility is chief among the capital virtues because it puts us in our proper place. It enables us to see where we stand in relation to God and others. It does not teach us to ignore ourselves but shows us how to view ourselves rightly.

—

Pride is an emotion, but it is also a disposition. An emotion is fleeting, but disposition is not. An emotion is a flash of feeling that will eventually dissipate. A disposition is a persistent bent toward a particular pattern of thinking or behavior. The deeply ingrained nature of sin means we will not be able to change our disposition toward sinful pride by force of will alone. We need something far stronger. The only solution for sinful pride is the same remedy required for all the deadly sins. It is the remedy of the cross. The entrance of sin into human experience means the sinful pride is part of our fallen constitution. We cannot rehabilitate it. Sinful pride must be put to death by the power of the Holy Spirit (Rom. 8:13; Col. 3:5). The way to overcome sinful pride is to displace this natural disposition with a different mentality. Using the word *displace* rather than *replace* is necessary because our sinful nature will only be fully eradicated in eternity. Jesus dealt a final death blow to sin on the cross, but the full effect of His redeeming work will not be felt by us until eternity.

Philippians 2:5 characterizes this new disposition as an "attitude" or "mindset" that is the same as that of Jesus Christ. The pattern of thinking and behavior that is the antithesis of sinful pride is simply stated: think as Jesus thought and do what Jesus did. In verses 6–11, Paul describes Christ's descent from glory into humility and His subsequent restoration and exaltation. Jesus' humility was grounded in a secure understanding of His position of equality with God. It was not something to be denied, but neither was it something to which He needed to cling. It was no stretch for Jesus to claim equality with God, and because He was not overreaching, it was no loss to take to Himself "the very nature of a servant" by being "made in human likeness" (v. 7).

Sinful pride is grasping and protective. It is not enough for the proud person to hold a position or achieve something; they crave recognition. We find the security we need to displace this natural tendency by grounding our hunger for recognition in our union with Christ. Our union with Christ in His saving work has secured our position. God has "raised us up with Christ and seated us with him in the heavenly realms in Christ Jesus, in order that in the coming ages he might show the incomparable riches of his grace, expressed in his kindness to us in Christ Jesus" (Eph. 2:6–7). We are not climbing; we are resting. Those who are in Christ do not need to compete with one another to win God's approval or gain Christ's affection.

Just as Jesus "emptied" Himself by refusing to claim the glory and prerogatives that were His by right, we displace our natural pride by denying our natural tendency to demand the acclaim that we believe is our due. This does not mean that we no longer feel it. It means that we must make it a point not to demand it. Jesus' obedience to the point of death empowers us in these "little" deaths of ours. Because Jesus made Himself "nothing," we find that we also can endure the discomfiture that comes with being nothing.

We must also follow Christ in the positive aspects of His humiliation. We do this by shifting the focus of our interest from ourselves to others. As Paul puts it, "in humility value others above yourselves, not looking to your own interests but each of you to the interests of the others" (Phil. 2:3–4). Jesus' humility didn't come from a sense of insignificance. His humility arose from an understanding of His greatness. It grew out of the certainty that His hand was the one in control of the spinning galaxies that make the rest of us feel small and insignificant.

More importantly, Jesus' humility was rooted in the knowledge that His Father's hand was in control of the events that swirled around Him and were about to engulf His very life.

It was this confidence that enabled Jesus to perform the task of a common servant and wash the disciples' feet on the night of His betrayal: "Jesus knew that the Father had put all things under his power, and that he had come from God and was returning to God; so he got up from the meal, took off his outer clothing, and wrapped a towel around his waist" (John 13:3–4). Jesus didn't cling to equality with God. He didn't hang on to it like some treasure that had to be pried from His hands. Instead, He laid aside the glory and privileges of divinity and took upon Himself a human nature. When you have already stooped that low, the distance from heaven's throne to the disciples' feet isn't much farther.

Foot washing was the job of a common household servant. That's why, before performing it, Jesus adopted the garb of a slave. Imagine the embarrassed hush that must have fallen as the disciples watched Jesus rise from the table and strip down to his loincloth. He wraps a towel around his waist and pours water into a basin. The disciples begin to eye one another uncomfortably. Everybody knows that they still have the dust of the road on their feet. Someone has to take the role of a servant and wash them before the Passover feast can start, but who wants that job? So they sit, each one hoping that someone else will take the initiative.

But there is something else making the disciples uncomfortable. It is the knowledge that there is tension simmering beneath the surface. They have just had a disagreement with one another about which of them should be considered the greatest (Luke 22:24). Perhaps that's the reason no one moves to take up the basin and towel. No one wants to give ground. Now here is Jesus, kneeling before them. Pouring water over their feet and drying them with the towel around his waist. They flush red with embarrassment as Jesus moves down the line. No one dares to speak. Until, at last, He comes to Peter, who all this time has been fuming. He can hardly believe what Jesus has done. Even worse is the fact that the other disciples just sat there and let Him do it. But Peter knows how to put a stop to that. "Lord, are you going to wash my feet?" Peter demands. Jesus urges Peter to be patient. "You do not realize now what I am doing, but later you will understand."

Peter will have none of it. "No, you shall never wash my feet," he firmly declares. Jesus' reply is just as firm. "Unless I wash you, you have no part with me." This breaks Peter's resolve, but not his pride. "Then, Lord," Peter replies, "not just my feet but my hands and my head as well!"

Peter exhibited a kind of false humility both when he objected to Jesus' action and then later when he demanded that Jesus wash his whole body (John 13:6–9). Each demand was intended to underscore Peter's unworthiness. In reality they revealed Peter's lack of self-awareness. Peter misunderstood the nature of his own need as well as Christ's intent—Peter unwittingly turned what Jesus had done inside out. Instead of being all about Jesus, for a brief moment, it suddenly became all about Peter. This was Peter proving that he was a cut above the rest. That is the chief problem with false humility. It is pride attempting to go incognito by putting on an ugly mask. But that mask is itself an expression of pride. Its aim is to draw attention to itself. Even when pride masquerades as humility, it does not take long before its true character becomes apparent to all.

Peter's question in John 13:6 betrays his thinking. As he watched Jesus wash the other disciples' feet, Peter seems to have thought, *We ought to be washing His feet!* But Peter wasn't washing Jesus' feet. He wasn't washing the other disciples' feet, either. For that matter, Peter hadn't even bothered to wash his own feet! Peter's neglect of the obvious is a reminder that we can be so focused on "the great thing" that we ignore the common task that lies at hand. At this particular moment, what was needed by the disciples was not greatness but the ability to use a basin of water and a towel. The disciples had that. What they lacked was a willingness to exercise that basic ability. Acts of humility do not have to be extreme. They are often as simple as holding the door for someone or keeping your opinion to yourself. Humility isn't just minding your own business; it is also tending to business. Do your job. Fulfill your obligations. Pay your taxes. Romans 13:7 commands, "Give to everyone what you owe them: If you owe taxes, pay taxes; if revenue, then revenue; if respect, then respect; if honor, then honor" (Rom. 13:7). Pride seeks glory, but humility is satisfied with the respect that comes from living your daily life in a responsible way (1 Thess. 4:11–12). In most cases, our humility is demonstrated through ordinary actions that are as basic as making the bed or removing the dirty dishes from the table. It is simply a matter of tending to the need at hand.

If Jesus' actions show us that humility requires "laying aside" our position to serve others, Peter's response shows us our most humbling moments may be when we are on the receiving end of someone else's service. There is a great irony in Jesus' action. In a sense, Jesus has given the disciples the very thing they think they wanted. They wanted honor and glory. They wanted recognition. They wanted to be treated like "somebody." Now the King of the Universe bows at their feet, serving them as if He were the slave and they were kings.

It is a mistake to associate humility with extreme demonstrations of self-abasement. This view confuses humility with humiliation. Like the fawning denials of Uriah Heep, such acts are only disguised forms of boasting. The discipline of humility involves any worthy action that undermines pride's lust for preeminence. Humility's chief characteristic is that it demonstrates a responsible interest in other people. The disciplines of humility are infused with compassion instead of self-loathing (Phil. 2:1).

C. S. Lewis called pride "the great sin" and observed that humility is not what we think it is. "Do not imagine that if you meet a really humble man he will be what most people call 'humble' nowadays: he will not be a sort of greasy, smarmy person, who is always telling that, of course, he is nobody," Lewis warns. "Probably all you will think about him is that he seemed a cheerful, intelligent chap who took a real interest in what *you* said to *him*."[9]

Some time ago, I saw a billboard for a university that promised its programs would turn the school's graduates into "conquerors." Conquerors was not a word I had expected. It seemed to me that a different description might have been more appropriate. Competent comes to mind. Or perhaps capable. Or maybe even hirable, as long as it is combined with the additional qualifying phrase: "in certain fields and economic environments."

The trouble with a school advertising that its graduates will be conquerors is that it is promising too much. It might be appropriate if the school specialized in military strategy and its students were preparing to be despots or generals. But even then, I think I would be suspicious. This billboard is an example of the kind of hyperbole we often hear in our marketed culture.

Should we expect to be conquerors? In one sense, the answer to this question is yes. Romans 8:37 assures believers that "in all these things we are more than conquerors through him who loved us." But when you look at the previous verse, it soon becomes clear that the conquering life Paul promises is not a life of glory and recognition. Rather, it is one that often includes trouble, hardship, persecution, want, and danger. By His blood, Jesus has made us "a kingdom and priests to serve His God and Father" (Rev. 1:6). We are destined for thrones in eternity. We will reign on the earth (Rev. 5:10). It is not wrong for us to look forward to a time when the glory that was lost to us when Adam fell will be restored. We may rightly "boast in the hope of the glory of God" (Rom. 5:2). But until that day Jesus Christ has secured for us an even more glorious name by which we must live. It is a title that Jesus has claimed for Himself. It is also the name by which we will be known in eternity. One day, we will be kings, but Christ has called us servants.

Pride

QUESTIONS FOR DISCUSSION:

1. Is pride ever a good thing? When is it a sin?

2. How would you define humility?

3. Do you think a truly humble person knows that they are humble? Why or why not?

CHAPTER 9

Yet Not I:
Separating Ourselves from Sin

S in is an abstraction until it shows up in our lives. Even though we have been forgiven, it is still a very present reality. To use Paul's language, when we want to obey God, sin is right there with us (Rom. 7:21). We want to be pure in heart, but we look a little too long in the wrong direction. We try to be generous but never seem to have anything to give to the poor. We would like to be happy about our colleague's promotion, but can't help feeling that it should have gone to us. Someone hurts us, but we don't get mad, we get even. The list goes on and on. If there are Ten Commandments, there are an almost infinite number of ways to violate them. Especially if sin involves intent as well as action, as Jesus teaches in the Sermon on the Mount (Matt. 5:21–30).

We are sometimes surprised at our capacity for sin. How is it possible for such thoughts and feelings to arise within our hearts? How could we have acted so badly? The apostle Paul describes this inner conflict in personal and vivid terms: "I do not understand what I do. For what I want to do I do not do, but what I hate I do" (Rom. 7:15). Theologians may disagree about whether this describes Paul's experience before or after his encounter with Christ, yet anyone who has struggled with sin can recognize his note of dismay. We have learned by painful experience that it is not enough to want to do good. Even when there is a will to obey, sin exerts a powerful counterforce that has the potential to undermine and sabotage our good intentions. The road to hell really *is* paved with good intentions. It is no wonder that the struggle in Paul produced the anguished cry of Romans 7:24, "What a wretched man I am! Who will rescue me from this body that is subject to death?"

How are we to cope with such a condition? With our other dysfunctions, we often respond with denial. We cover up our problems, dressing them in nice clothes and giving them respectable names. As we have seen in the previous chapters, we do the same with sin. Another coping strategy is to detach ourselves intellectually and emotionally from our own sin and turn it into an abstraction. Theology lends itself to detachment and abstraction. Theologians tend to hold ideas at arm's length when considering them. Maybe this is because some of the church's early theologians, despite Tertullian's assertion that Athens and Jerusalem are poles apart, saw philosophy as a friend to their thinking and maybe even as a distant relative.[1] Theologians seem to have an affection for abstract systems. Or maybe it is the result of the ideas themselves. Theological abstraction is what happens when we speak of heavenly realities in earthly language.

When it comes to the theology of sin, however, there is an additional incentive to keep things in the abstract. Abstraction allows us to maintain our emotional distance from sin's harsh reality as we catalog and organize its effects. We list the various sins and categorize them. Some theologians formulate taxonomies of sin, arranging them by weight or penalty the way an entomologist divides the insect world into kingdom, phylum, and class. The emotional distance this creates may be helpful, perhaps even necessary, if we are to think about sin. But this kind of analysis also has a flattening effect. It is the difference between seeing a two-dimensional picture of a corpse and handling its cold, slack limbs or breathing its scent as it putrefies.

Yet as familiar as sin is to us, we cannot help feeling a natural distance from it. Our relationship to sin is an intimate one, as one might expect with something that is "in me" (Rom. 7:8, 17). It arises within our own hearts (James 1:13–15). It is part of our nature (Eph. 2:3). At the same time, sin is an alien presence introduced into the human race from the outside. Since the fall, every descendant of Adam has been born into sin, but humanity was not created sinful. At our worst moments (or maybe I should say even at our best), we cannot help feeling that something is out of order. The Scriptures make it clear that the damage done by the entrance of sin into human nature is so extensive that every part is affected. Sin is more than a weakening of human goodness; it is an absence. Paul confessed, "I know that good itself does not dwell in me, that is, in my sinful nature" (Rom. 7:18). Ever since

Adam's fall, the impetus toward good that was a feature of our original creation has been supplanted by sin that now dwells in our nature, but the impetus remains.

The apostle calls this impetus a "desire to do good" in Romans 7:18 and also refers to it "the law of my mind," an impulse that "delights" in his "inner being" in the law of God (Rom. 7:22, 23). I am not saying that in every bad person there is a good person trying to get out. Yet there is in every person a memory of the good. This memory is fragile and is easily suppressed. It can also be distorted so that not everyone agrees on the standard. But its greatest weakness of this will to do good is that sin has robbed it of its power. The will may exist but it is easily overpowered by indwelling sin. As a result, when I want to do good, I find instead that sin is right there with me, "waging war against the law of my mind and making me a prisoner of the law of sin at work within me" (Rom. 7:23). Notice that Paul speaks of this warring force as a law.

In fact, Paul talks about three laws that define this struggle with sin. First is the law of God, the commandments that provide the boundaries and show us the shape of what is good. This law includes not only the Ten Commandments found in the law of Moses but the myriad of expectations and obligations that God's standard of righteousness lays upon us. These commandments were "intended to bring life," but sin's domineering presence in us has the opposite effect (Rom. 7:10–11). When the commandment comes, sin springs to life and puts us to death. Second is the law of the mind or the will to do good. This is our answering cry of agreement with God. It is what C. S. Lewis called "the law of human nature" (see chapter 1). The law of the mind is the

"Amen" of our conscience, which agrees with God's assessment of what is right and what is wrong. Not only is it a memory of the good, it is ultimately a memory of what may be known about God Himself that leaves the sinner without excuse (Rom. 1:19–20). The law of the mind is the standard that informs the conscience, our thoughts sometimes accusing us, and maybe even at other times even defending our actions (Rom. 2:15).

Here, then, is our dilemma when it comes to virtue or what Paul calls "the good." We can aspire, but we cannot execute. The power of the law of sin at work in us, the third law, is so dominating that our performance is spotty at best. Our obedience is not thorough or consistent enough to claim the status of "righteous," as God defines righteousness. Even if we could, we would still bear the burden of the guilt that has been laid upon us because of Adam's disobedience. As a result, God's law, although intended for our good, inevitably becomes an agent of death, and the deficiency is with us. Without another way open to us, we must be forever divided, servants of two masters but obedient to only one, the law of sin (Rom. 7:25).

There is another way open to us. It is a fourth law that serves as God's comprehensive answer to our struggle with sin and righteousness. It is called "law of the Spirit who gives life" and it is the only force that is able to overcome the law of sin and death that is at work in us (Rom. 8:1–2). This new law is imparted to the believer by the Father, Son, and Holy Spirit working in concert by the threefold actions of justification, regeneration, and sanctification. These three actions are distinct but also inseparable from one another in the believer's experience of salvation. They begin with justification, which is "the judicial act or sentence of God, by which the sinner is declared to be entitled, in consideration of what Christ has done on his behalf, to the favor of God, and of which sanctification is the efficient execution; and the term regeneration is confined to the initial efficient act by which the new life is imparted, of which sanctification is the progressive development."[2] Of these three, justification and regeneration are momentary, while sanctification is progressive. Regeneration and justification happen once and are not repeated. They do not increase in their scope. As far as God's declaration goes, we are as righteous as we will ever be. All the life that Christ promised to us is imparted instantaneously so that the Scriptures speak of those who are in Christ as "alive with Christ" (Eph. 2:5; Col. 2:13).

Like sanctification, sin is also progressive. Because sin comes to us through Adam, the guilt is instantaneous. But the experience and practice of sin are expansive. We are born sinners. No one has to teach us how to sin. Yet as we age, we also become more accomplished in the practice of sin. Or perhaps it may be better to say that sin is restrictive and that sanctification expands us. "The person who reaches toward God and wants to please God gets, so to speak, stretched by this move, and ennobled by the transcendence of its object," theologian Cornelius Plantinga explains. "But the person who curves in on himself, who wants God's gifts without God, who wants to satisfy the desires of a divided heart, ends up sagging and contracting into a little wad."[3]

Similarly, like sanctification, sin also has a cooperative dimension. We collaborate with our fallen nature and thereby add to the guilt that comes to us through Adam. We are born sinners, and we also willingly choose to sin. But here also there is an important difference when it comes to sanctification. We cooperate with sin, but the nature of our relationship with sin is not entirely voluntary. The language Scripture uses to describe our relationship with sin is the language of slavery (Rom. 6:6, 20). Without the intervening grace of God, we cannot be anything other than slaves to sin. Scripture also uses the language of slavery to speak of the believer's relationship to righteousness but with an important difference. Our relationship to sin was one of involuntary servitude. We were "sold as a slave to sin" (Rom. 7:14). We cooperated with our sin nature because we had no other alternative. The grace that comes to us through Christ has transferred us to a new master but one who asks us to serve freely.

In other words, the practice of holiness, unlike the practice of sin, is not compulsory. Obedience is our obligation in Christ, but we are not forced to obey. The process of sanctification involves the daily choice to offer ourselves to God as servants of righteousness. There are two ways open to the Christian where formerly there was only one. This difference is more than a liberation of the will; it involves the expansion of our capability and the renewal of our desires. Not only does righteousness incline us to obey, the work of the Holy Spirit empowers that obedience. What God requires, He also performs. However, we should not view the righteous practice of the Christian life as an "add-on," something that we bring to the work of justification. Obedience is not our contribution to the work of Christ. Sanctification is not us doing our part now that Christ has done His. Sanctification is the work of God as much as justification.

God's comprehensive answer to our struggle with sin and righteousness is the gospel, with all its promises and effects. Paul captures the threefold nature of this gospel work of justification, regeneration, and sanctification in Romans 8:3–4: "For what the law was powerless to do because it was weakened by the flesh, God did by sending his own Son in the likeness of sinful flesh to be a sin offering. And so he condemned sin in the flesh, in order that the righteous requirement of the law might be fully met in us, who do not live according to the flesh but according to the Spirit." These verses speak of the work of the Father, Son, and Spirit in dealing with the guilt, penalty, and power of sin. The Father sends the Son in the likeness of sinful flesh to be a sacrifice. The Son, in turn, deals a death blow to sin's guilt and power by shedding His blood for us and rising from the dead. The Holy Spirit makes it possible to live a different kind of life. Instead of being limited to the impulses of the fallen nature, we now have the capacity to live "according to the Spirit."

The work of Christ does not eradicate sin's presence within our nature, this side of eternity. Instead, it introduces life where before there was only death. Neither does the cross erect an impermeable wall between the believer and sin. Sin may still seek to influence us, but it no longer owns us. Those who are in Christ have been given the upper hand in the struggle against sin because of the cross: "For we know that our old self was crucified with him so that the body ruled by sin might be done away with, that we should no longer be slaves to sin—because anyone who has died has been set free from sin" (Rom. 6:6–7).

The answer to the believer's ongoing struggle with sin is new life that comes to us through Christ. But the solution is also Christ's death. Sin's ongoing presence in the believer's life can be countered only by the cross. When sin attempts to reassert its dominance in our lives, we must "put to death" whatever belongs to our fallen nature (Col. 3:5). The cross is more than a historical event. Our union with Christ in His suffering means that it is also a power that we apply to the law of sin that dwells within us. This is not magic or even mysticism. It is the exercise of faith. To use the accounting language that Paul employs in Romans 6:11, separating ourselves from the sin that dwells within us begins with an act of reckoning, by which we count ourselves to be dead to sin. Resistance to the impulses of the sinful nature is an act of faith because it takes God at His word. Scripture tells us that our sinful nature has been crucified with Christ. Resistance to sin and the positive obedience that goes with it are acts of faith that are grounded in the saving work of Christ and the enabling power of the Spirit. Any act of obedience must be grounded in the gospel because God's acceptance of our effort depends upon the righteousness of Christ. The effectiveness of our effort to do what is right relies upon the empowerment of the Holy Spirit.

———

Several years ago, I met a man who worked with alcoholics at an area rescue mission. He spoke about the challenge of working with those whose lives had been ravaged by sin. Then, after a pause, he shook his head and said, "You know, we sing a lot about victory around here, but we don't see much of it." Freedom from sin's mastery does not mean that Christians cannot become entangled in sin. It is still possible for those who are no longer slaves to sin to engage in a kind of voluntary servitude to their old master by obeying the impulses of their sin nature (Rom. 6:16).

The apostle highlights the gravity of sin when he warns that the unrighteous will not inherit the kingdom of God: "Do not be deceived: Neither the sexually immoral nor idolaters nor adulterers nor men who have sex with men nor thieves nor the greedy nor drunkards nor slanderers nor swindlers will inherit the kingdom of God" (1 Cor. 6:9–10). Yet he also holds out the hope for forgiveness and transformation when he adds, "And that is what some of you were. But you were washed, you were sanctified, you were justified in the name of the Lord Jesus Christ and by the Spirit of our God" (1 Cor. 6:11). There is victory over sin through the power of the cross. But victory in Jesus does not preclude struggle or even failure. Neither does it immunize us from the appeal of temptation. Long-standing patterns of bondage do not automatically disappear when we trust in Christ. Those who have been raised in abusive or addictive family systems may spend the rest of their lives battling patterns of thinking and behavior that are the collateral damage of sin. Those who have been deeply embedded in a lifestyle of sexual immorality, whether it is heterosexual or homosexual, often continue to feel the tug of desire, even after they have believed the gospel. The alcoholic may still want to take a drink, and the addict may feel the pull of their favorite drug of choice. Paul's reminder to the Corinthians that certain behaviors are incompatible with the believer's calling in grace implies that some in the church needed the reminder.

There is victory in Jesus, but the sentimentalized rhetoric that the church sometimes uses to speak about that victory often gives the impression that victory over sin is instantaneous and easily won. This romanticized view of sin does not prepare people for the rigors of following Jesus. The church's sentimentalization of sin tends to take two forms. One is to understate the difficulty that believers face when turning from their sin. The other is to minimize sin's seriousness or to dismiss it altogether. Those who understate the challenges that face us when we turn away from our sin offer a faulty vision of the Christian life that gives the impression that the impulses of the sinful nature will simply disappear. Or, if those impulses remain, one merely needs to take them to the altar and pray away any besetting sin.

Certainly, prayer is an important strategy when dealing with sin and temptation. In Gethsemane, Jesus urged His disciples, "Watch and pray so that you will not fall into temptation. The spirit is willing, but the flesh is weak" (Matt. 26:41). Prayer is our first line of defense when it comes to temptation, but action is also needed. One of the most common strategies recommended by Scripture for dealing with temptation is to flee. Paul told the Corinthians to flee sexual immorality and idolatry (1 Cor. 6:18; 10:14). He warned Timothy to flee the evil desires of youth (2 Tim. 2:22). Some who have been praying about their sinful desires wonder why God hasn't taken them away. They have it backward. They wrongly assume that God will deliver them from sin by eliminating desire. Instead, He expects them to move away from the sins they have come to love and to learn that they can live an abundant life in Christ with their desires unfulfilled.

Others sentimentalize sin by minimizing it or redefining it. This approach is a form of false compassion. It attempts to make things easier for those who are troubled with sin by making their sins permissible. Where Scripture calls some desire or action sinful, the sentimentalist blunts the force of this assessment by noting that we all sin. Universal failure amounts to permission. It is also common to legitimize certain sin by treating them as a pre-existing condition or inclination. This overly simplistic reasoning argues that if we are born with a certain predilection, we are meant to act upon it. Where the Bible disagrees, as in the case of sexual preference and sexual identity, the sentimentalist appeals to a more enlightened understanding of what the Bible says.

Forgiveness and God's gift of righteousness are instantaneous and received without cost to us. Obedience to Christ's call to follow, however, comes at a cost (Matt. 16:24; Luke 14:28). New life in Christ often demands the restructuring of discipleship to replace old habits with new. Many of the images the Bible uses to speak of discipleship imply that it involves a measure of rigor, struggle, and even loss. Jesus speaks of the disciple's life as the way of the cross: "Whoever wants to be my disciple must deny themselves and take up their cross daily and follow me" (Luke 9:23). Paul urged Timothy to endure hardship like a soldier of Christ. He also compared the rigors of the Christian life to the discipline of an athlete and the hard work of a farmer (2 Tim. 2:3–6).

When it comes to the believer's battle against temptation, the victory is Christ's, but the struggle is ours. Applying the power of the cross to the impulses of our sinful nature is comfortable only after the cross has done its work. When we are tempted, we do not have to look far to find a way out. 1 Corinthians 10:13 promises, "No temptation has overtaken you except what is common to mankind. And God is faithful; he will not let you be tempted beyond what you can bear. But when you are tempted, he will also provide a way out so that you can endure it." Yet this assurance also implies a measure of discomfort and struggle.

The cross is not a magic wand that makes temptation disappear. Grace is not God's fairy dust that makes all our problems and struggles disappear. The cross is an instrument of death, and when we apply its power to our sinful nature, we experience a kind of death. We feel the compelling draw of sinful desire, but we refuse to gratify it. We do not get what we want. Our hunger goes unsatisfied. We would prefer to have more but settle for less. Rather than opting for the wide and easy way, we enter the narrow gate and follow the hard path. Instead of getting even, we take the hit and suffer the loss. We do not give in to the sense of outrage we feel when someone else gets what we think we deserve, but practice the painful discipline of wishing them well. We follow Christ in the path of downard mobility by taking on the role of a servant. Paul's promise is true. When sin comes in, Jesus provides a way out. The way out is always the way of the cross.

Virtue always demands effort. But virtue begins with faith. Growth in virtue involves initiative and effort on our part, but it cannot rightly be called an achievement. We must be made good in order to do good. As Jesus starkly noted, "No one is good—except God alone" (Mark 10:18). *Sanctification* is the word that theologians use to speak of the believer's journey into virtue. But we should not think of the way of virtue as a matter of living up to God's standard of righteousness. It is the Spirit-empowered practice of living out the righteousness that has already been given to us as a gift.

Our journey into virtue begins when we come to recognize, as Paul does in Romans 7:17, that the sinful dimension of our nature is not our true self. There is more to us than the sin that stirs within our flesh. The real me is the redeemed me. Washed by the blood of Christ and empowered by the Holy Spirit, we have been granted the separation from sin that comes by grace. Jesus Christ has removed sin's guilt by taking the penalty upon Himself. His cross has shattered sin's power. Sin may still seek to influence me but it no longer owns me. As Paul observes in 1 Corinthians 15:10, "But by the grace of God I am what I am, and his grace to me was not without effect. No, I worked harder than all of them—yet not I, but the grace of God that was with me."

Where sin is concerned, the cross has brought about a separation. It is God's agent of manumission, freeing us from slavery to sin's power. But where righteousness is concerned, grace has a different effect. It introduces a new "law" within me—"the law of the Spirit who gives life" (Rom. 8:2). This is the Spirit who binds me to Christ and works within me. His power is the counterforce that enables me to resist sin's continuing attempt to draw me in. I can say yes to God. Yet not I, but the grace of God that is with me.

QUESTIONS FOR DISCUSSION:

1. What does the Bible mean when it says that those who belong to Christ are dead to sin?

2. If we are dead to sin, why does it sometimes seem so alive?

3. How does the Holy Spirit enable us to have victory over sin? What does victory look like in your personal experience?

Epilogue

According to family legend, my great-grandfather was the first one to drive the twenty-mule team out of Death Valley loaded with Borax. I have no idea whether this is true. I suspect that it is a work of fiction, like most family legends. But I liked to recount this story to my friends when I was growing up since the twenty-mule team was featured in commercials on the popular television show *Death Valley Days*. It made me feel just short of famous.

Borax is a "detergent booster." It's used in a lot of other things too: fertilizer, rocket fuel, and automobile windshields, just to name a few. But I always thought of it as soap. The same people who made Borax also made Boraxo, the hand detergent that promised to make hands "soft, smooth, and really clean."

Cleanliness seemed to be the driving concern of most of the commercials we watched in those days. They fretted about clean clothes, clean floors, and clear complexions. What did this say about us as a culture? Were we especially dirty? Maybe we were just fastidious. Perhaps it was a little of both.

At points, the Bible seems similarly obsessed. The Old Testament, in particular, appears to be especially concerned about matters of cleanness and uncleanness with its detailed regulations about food, clothing, and its peculiar stipulations regarding spots and blemishes. When we read through these laws, we do not get the impression that what is at issue is primarily a matter of hygiene. Indeed, some of the measures prescribed do not seem hygienic at all, especially when the "cleansing" agent is blood. Something else is going on. The New Testament writer of Hebrews admits as much by calling such measures a "shadow" that can never perfect those who repeat them year after year. Instead of being a remedy, they were a reminder of sin (Heb. 10:1–3).

In this book, we have been looking at the capital sins. One danger of cataloging sin in this way is that it may tempt us to approach the problem sin atomistically. We may concentrate only on particular sins or specific techniques but fail to address the problem at its root. As we have seen, the Bible has much to say about each of the seven deadly sins. But its ultimate remedy is more comprehensive. God's solution for sin involves more than spot cleaning. The cleanness that Jesus grants is one that begins on the inside and works its way out. Most of the cleansing with which we are familiar works the other way around. The solution to our sin problem is not a matter of *getting* clean but *being* clean. Only Christ's blood can do that for us: "God made him who had no sin to be sin for us, so that in him we might become the righteousness of God" (2 Cor. 5:21).

If you don't know where to begin, start here. Look to Jesus to make you clean on the inside. Accept the gift of righteousness that God offers through faith in Him. Then trust God to carry out the work of transformation by His Spirit. As you rely on the

Spirit's power to obey and look to God's Word for guidance, you will also learn how to live in a world that calls evil good and good evil.

When Jesus sent His disciples into the world, He knew that He was sending them out like sheep among wolves and warned them of the need to live shrewdly (Matt. 10:16). Shrewd living requires vigilance. It demands that we become holy skeptics who do not automatically believe that everything that the world around us calls good is good. More than anything else, such a life requires that we take God at His word and allow Him to show us the true shape of virtue.

Before they were called Christians, those who followed Jesus were called "the Way" (Acts 9:2; 19:9; 22:4). This label implies that there is more to the Christian faith than a set of beliefs. Christianity is a way of life, the way of the one who is Himself the way, the truth, and the life (John 14:6). Yet there is also more to being a Christian than imitation. Lean too far toward imitation, and we reduce the faith to grim moralism. Make Christianity only a set of propositions, and the vitality of what we believe disappears in a fog of theological abstractions or pious slogans. As stated earlier, Christian living isn't just a way of life; it is the way of the living. It is the character of life exhibited by those who have been made alive by Christ. "Jesus is clear that his truth, that truth that is the way and the life, is himself," William Willimon observes. "We really have no idea what the truth is, living as we do in a culture of lies, had not Jesus shown us a life that is true to God."[1]

Willimon goes on to say that we cannot know the truth

before we have been made truthful. In the same way, we cannot understand virtue before we have been made virtuous. Virtue has its beginning and end in Jesus Christ. He is the way to virtue. Jesus is the one who shatters our denial about sin and opens our eyes so that we know what true virtue looks like. He is the life, whose forgiveness and empowering grace make a life of virtue possible for us. If you don't know where to begin when it comes to dealing with the problem of sin, begin with Jesus. He is God's remedy for sin.

Acknowledgments

I am grateful to Drew Dyck, acquisitions editor at Moody Publishers, for his interest and help with this project. It is a pleasure to be working once again with Kevin Emmert, who served as project editor. Their suggestions and editing have made this a better book. I am also very appreciative of my agent, Mark Sweeney, whose friendship and advocacy have meant so much to me over the years. Last but certainly not least, I want to say thank you to my wife, Jane, who is always my first editor, most enthusiastic cheerleader, and whose opinion I value more than any other.

Notes

Chapter 1: Sin and the Seven Dangerous Virtues

1. Bob Smietana, "Two-Thirds of Americans Say They Are Sinners," *Christianity Today*, August, 15, 2017, https://www.christianitytoday.com/news/2017/august/most-americans-admit-sinners-romans-3-for-all-have-sinned.html.

2. Owen Chadwick, *Western Asceticism* (Philadelphia: Westminster John Knox, 1958), 43.

3. Os Guinness, *Steering Through Chaos: Vice and Virtue in an Age of Moral Confusion* (Colorado Springs: NavPress, 2000), 21.

4. Cornelius Plantinga Jr., *Not the Way It's Supposed to Be: A Breviary of Sin* (Grand Rapids: Eerdmans, 1995), 13.

5. John Murray, *Principles of Conduct: Aspects of Biblical Ethics* (Grand Rapids: Eerdmans, 1957), 176.

6. Charles Taylor, *Sources of the Self* (Cambridge, MA: Harvard University Press, 1989), 4.

7. C. S. Lewis, *Mere Christianity* (New York: HarperOne, 2001), 3–4.

8. Ibid.

9. H. C. G. Moule, *Studies in Romans* (Grand Rapids: Kregel, 1977), 132.

10. Herman Ridderbos, *Paul: An Outline of His Theology* (Grand Rapids: Eerdmans, 1975), 103.

11. Plantinga Jr., *Not the Way it's Supposed to Be*, 47.

12. Mchael W. Holmes, *The Apostolic Fathers* (Grand Rapids: Baker, 2007), 345.

13. C. E. B. Cranfield, *The Epistle to the Romans, Vol. I* (Edinburgh: T & T Clark, 1975), 315.

14. John Calvin, *The Epistle of Paul the Apostle to the Hebrews and The First and Second Epistles of Peter*, trans. W. B. Johnston (Grand Rapids: Eerdmans, 1963), 329.

15. G. C. Berkouwer, *Sin* (Grand Rapids: Eerdmans, 1971), 285.

Chapter 2: Love—*The Seduction of Desire*

1. Joe McDonald, quoted in Sheila Weller, "Suddenly That Summer," *Vanity Fair*, June 14, 2012, https://www.vanityfair.com/culture/2012/07/lsd-drugs-summer-of-love-sixties.

2. Dale Kuehne in an interview with Ken Myers in *Mars Hill Audio Journal*, vol. 99, 2013.

3. Jean Kilbourne, "So Sexy So Soon," Wellesley Centers for Women, *Research & Action Report* 30, no. 2 (Spring/Summer 2009): 12, https://www.wcwonline.org/images/stories/researchandaction/pdf/rar_springsummer2009.pdf.

4. Ibid., 13.

5. Helmut Thielicke, *Being Human . . . Becoming Human* (Garden City, NY: Doubleday, 1984), 189.

6. Ibid., 191.

7. Dale S. Kuehne, *Sex and the iWorld: Rethinking Relationship beyond an Age of Individualism* (Grand Rapids: Baker, 2009), 74.

8. Wendell Berry, *Sex, Economy, Freedom & Community* (New York: Pantheon, 1992), 119.

9. Dorothy Sayers, *Letters to a Diminished Church* (Nashville: Nelson, 2004), 75.

10. Martyn Lloyd-Jones, *Studies in the Sermon on the Mount* (Grand Rapids: Eerdmans, 1979), 237.

11. Sayers, *Letters to a Diminished Church*, 77.

12. C. S. Lewis, *The Four Loves* (New York: Harcourt Brace Jovanovich, 1960), 183–84.

13. Henry Fairlie, *The Seven Deadly Sins Today* (Notre Dame, IN: University of Notre Dame, 1979), 185.

14. John Stott, *The Message of Galatians* (Downers Grove, IL: InterVarsity Press, 1968), 151.

15. C. S. Lewis, *The Weight of Glory and Other Addresses* (New York: Macmillan, 1980), 3–4.

Chapter 3: Satisfaction—*Coping with the Hunger That Cannot Be Satisfied*

1. Owen Chadwick, *Western Asceticism* (Philadelphia: Westminster John Knox, 1958), 317.
2. Ibid., 318.
3. Ibid., 51.
4. Dallas Willard, *The Spirit of the Disciplines: Understanding How God Changes Lives* (San Francisco: Harper, 1988), 166.
5. Ibid.
6. ANAD, Eating Disorder Statistics, https://anad.org/education-and-awareness/about-eating-disorders/eating-disorders-statistics/.
7. "Alcohol Use Disorder," National Institute on Alcohol Abuse and Alcoholism, https://www.niaaa.nih.gov/alcohol-health/overview-alcohol-consumption/alcohol-use-disorders.
8. Lynne Gerber, "Fat Christians and Fit Elites: Negotiating Class and Status in Evangelical Weight-Loss Culture," *American Quarterly* 64, no. 1 (2012): 63.
9. Jean Kilbourne, *Can't Buy My Love: How Advertising Changes the Way We Think and Feel* (New York: Simon & Schuster, 1999), 115.
10. Ibid., 27.
11. Wendell Berry, *The Art of the Commonplace: The Agrarian Essays of Wendell Berry* (Berkeley, CA: Counterpoint, 2002), 326.
12. C. S. Lewis, *The Screwtape Letters* (New York: Macmillan, 1978), 77.
13. Os Guinness, *Steering Through Chaos: Vice and Virtue in an Age of Moral Confusion* (Colorado Spring: NavPress, 2000), 213.
14. "Food Deserts in America (Infographic)," Tulane University School of Social Work, May 10, 2018, https://socialwork.tulane.edu/blog/food-deserts-in-america.
15. Joachim Jeremias, *New Testament Theology* (New York: Scribners, 1971), 200.
16. Andrew B. McGowan, *Ancient Christian Worship: Early Church Practices in Social, Historical, and Theological Perspective* (Grand Rapids: Baker, 2014), 20.
17. Berry, *The Art of the Commonplace*, 323.
18. Ibid.
19. Willard, *The Spirit of the Disciplines*, 166.
20. Ibid., 159.
21. Berry, *The Art of the Commonplace*, 323.

Chapter 4: Prosperity—*Why Wanting More Means We Will Never Have Enough*

1. Stanley Hauerwas, *The Hauerwas Reader* (Durham, NC: Duke, 2001), 381.
2. Dorothy Sayers, *Letters to a Diminished Church* (Nashville: Thomas Nelson, 2004), 87.
3. Ibid.
4. Charles C. Brooks, "Powerbull: The Lottery Loves Poverty," *The Wall Street Journal*, August 27, 2017, https://www.wsj.com/articles/powerbull-the-lottery-loves-poverty-1503868287.
5. Samuel T. Wilkinson, "Medical and Recreational Marijuana: Commentary and Review of the Literature," *Missouri Medicine* 110, no. 6 (2013): 524–28.
6. Josef Pieper, *Happiness & Contemplation* (South Bend, IN: St. Augustine's Press, 1979), 26.
7. Helmut Thielicke, *Life Can Begin Again* (Philadelphia: Fortress, 1963), 9.
8. Eugene Peterson, *A Long Obedience in the Same Direction* (Downers Grove, IL: InterVarsity, 1980), 112.

Chapter 5: Leisure—*Living Beyond the Weekend*

1. Os Guinness, *Steering Through Chaos: Vice and Virtue in an Age of Moral Confusion* (Colorado Springs: NavPress, 2000), 151.
2. Joe Pinsker, "How Much Leisure Time Do the Happiest People Have?" *The Atlantic*, February 21, 2019, https://www.theatlantic.com/family/archive/2019/02/free-time-life-satisfaction/583171/.
3. Neil Postman, *Technopoly: The Surrender of Culture to Technology* (New York: Vintage, 1992), 13.
4. "Average Hours Spent in Selected Activities by Employment Status and Sex," U.S. Bureau of Labor Statistics,https://www.bls.gov/charts/american-time-use/activity-by-emp.htm.
5. Rachel Krantz-Kent, "Television, Capturing America's Attention at Prime Time and Beyond," U.S. Bureau of Labor Statistics, *Beyond the Numbers* 7, no. 14 (September 2018): https://www.bls.gov/opub/btn/volume-7/television-capturing-americas-attention.htm.
6. Eugene Peterson, *Under the Unpredictable Plant: An Exploration in Vocational Holiness* (Grand Rapids: Eerdmans, 1994), 3.

7. Eugene Peterson, *Leap Over a Wall: Earthy Spirituality for Everyday Christians* (New York: HarperCollins, 1997), 30.
8. https://www.thegospelcoalition.org/sections/faith-work/.
9. Dorothy Sayers, *Letters to a Diminished Church* (Nashville: Thomas Nelson, 2004), 97.
10. Derek Thompson, "Workism Is Making Americans Miserable," *The Atlantic*, February 24, 2019, https://www.theatlantic.com/ideas/archive/2019/02/religion-workism-making-americans-miserable/583441/.
11. Ibid.
12. Martyn Lloyd-Jones, *Preaching and Preachers* (Grand Rapids: Zondervan, 1971), 9.
13. Josef Pieper, *Leisure: The Basis of Culture* (San Francisco: Ignatius, 1963), 46.

Chapter 6: Justice—*Life in an Age of Outrage*

1. Owen Chadwick, *Western Asceticism* (Philadelphia: Westminster John Knox, 1958) 53.
2. Britney Fitzgerald, "Bullying on Twitter: Researchers Find 15,000 Bully-Related Tweets Sent Daily," *HuffPost*, August 2, 2012, https://www.huffpost.com/entry/bullying-on-twitter_n_1732952.
3. Stefan Wojcik and Adam Hughes, "Sizing Up Twitter Users," Pew Research Center, April 24, 2019, https://www.pewresearch.org/internet/2019/04/24/sizing-up-twitter-users/.
4. Ryan Martin, "Why We Get Mad—and Why It's Healthy," TED, TEDxFondduLac, August 2018, https://www.ted.com/talks/ryan_martin_why_we_get_mad_and_why_it_s_healthy/transcript.
5. J. I. Packer, "God," in *The New Dictionary of Theology* (Downers Grove, IL: InterVarsity, 1988), 277.
6. C. S. Lewis, *Mere Christianity* (New York: HarperOne, 2001), 3.
7. Helmut Thielicke, *Christ and the Meaning of Life* (Cambridge: James Clark, 1965), 76.
8. Robert Robinson, "Come Thou Fount of Every Blessing," 1758.

Chapter 7: Envy—*Getting What's Coming to Them*

1. F. F. Bruce, *Commentary on Galatians* (Grand Rapids: Eerdmans, 1982), 249.

2. Os Guinness, *Steering Through Chaos: Vice and Virtue in an Age of Moral Confusion* (Colorado Springs: NavPress, 2000), 77.

3. Owen Chadwick, *Western Asceticism* (Philadelphia: Westminster John Knox, 1958), 277.

4. St. Basil, "Homily 11: Concerning Envy" in *The Fathers of the Church Vol. IX, St. Basil Ascetical Works* (Washington, DC: Catholic University of America Press, 1962), 463.

5. Ibid.

6. Owen Chadwick, *Western Asceticism*, 212.

7. James K. A. Smith, *Desiring the Kingdom* (Grand Rapids: Baker, 2009), 50–51.

8. Helmut Thielicke, *Life Can Begin Again* (Philadelphia: Fortress, 1963), 130.

9. Josef Pieper, *Happiness & Contemplation* (South Bend, IN: St. Augustine's Press, 1979), 26.

Chapter 8: Pride—*Why God Needs to Put Us in Our Place*

1. Jessica Tracy, *Take Pride: Why the Deadliest Sin Holds the Secret to Human Success* (Boston: Houghton Mifflin Harcourt, 2016), xii.

2. Ibid., 43.

3. Ibid., 58.

4. Ibid., 196.

5. Thomas à Kempis, *The Imitation of Christ* (New York: Image, 1955), 163.

6. Owen Chadwick, *Western Asceticism* (Philadelphia: Westminster John Knox, 1958), 212.

7. C. S. Lewis, *The Screwtape Letters* (New York: HarperOne, 1996), 22.

8. Charles Dickens, *The Personal History of David Copperfield* (London: Bradbury & Evans, 1850), 181.

9. C. S. Lewis, *Mere Christianity* (New York: HarperOne, 2001), 128.

Chapter 9: Yet Not I—*Separating Ourselves from Sin*

1. In *The Prescriptions Against the Heretics*, African theologian and apologist Tertullian wrote: "What has Jerusalem to do with Athens, the Church with the Academy, the Christian with the heretic? Our principles come from the Porch of Solomon, who had himself taught that

the Lord is to be sought in simplicity of heart." *Early Latin Theology*, ed. S. L. Greenslade (Philadelphia: Westminster, 1956), 36.

2. B. B. Warfield, "Sanctification," in *Selected Shorter Writings of Benjamin B. Warfield Vol. II*, ed. John E. Meeter, (Philippsburg, NJ: Presbyterian and Reformed, 1973), 325.

3. Cornelius Plantinga Jr., *Not the Way It's Supposed to Be: A Breviary of Sin* (Grand Rapids: Eerdmans, 1995), 62.

Epilogue

1. William H. Willimon, "Jesus' Peculiar Truth," *Christianity Today*, March 4, 1996, 22.

The present is more than a place where the past comes to rest.
It is more than a staging ground for the future.
The present is where God shows up.

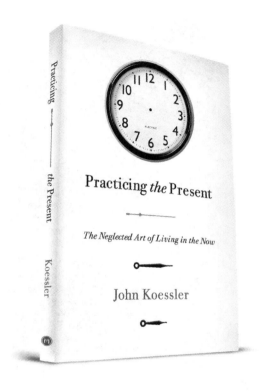

Practicing *the* Present

The Neglected Art of Living in the Now

John Koessler

MOODY
Publishers®

From the Word ***to Life***®

We want to change the past and control the future, but usually all we really do is exhaust ourselves in the here and now. Dr. John Koessler teaches you how to evade the tyranny of past regrets and future plans and meet God right where you are, in the present.

978-0-8024-1868-5 | also available as eBook and audiobook

WHAT TO DO WHEN THEY SAY THEY'RE CHRISTIAN BUT DON'T KNOW JESUS

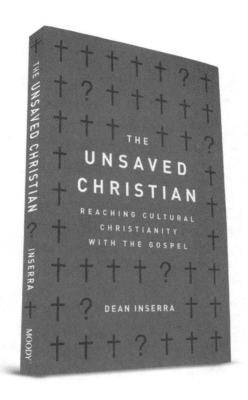

The Unsaved Christian equips you to confront cultural Christianity with honesty, compassion, and grace, whether you're doing it from the pulpit or the pews. If you've ever felt stuck or unsure how to minister to someone who identifies as Christian but still needs Jesus, this book is for you.

978-0-8024-1880-7 | also available as an eBook

STUDY THE BIBLE WITH PROFESSORS
FROM MOODY BIBLE INSTITUTE

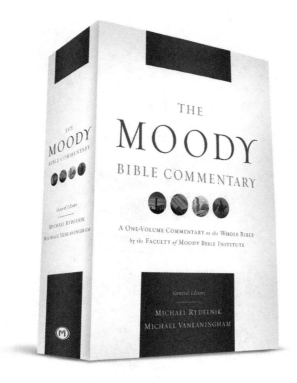

"What comes into our minds when we think about God is the most important thing about us."
—A. W. Tozer